The Stratification of Musical Rhythm

The Stratification
of
Musical Rhythm

Maury Yeston

New Haven and London, Yale University Press, 1976

Published with assistance from the foundation
established in memory of Calvin Chapin of the
Class of 1788, Yale College.

Library of Congress catalog card number: 75-18189
International standard book number: 0-300-01884-3

Designed by John O. C. McCrillis
and set in Baskerville type.
Printed in the United States of America by
Alpine Press, South Braintree, Massachusetts.

Published in Great Britain, Europe, and Africa by
Yale University Press, Ltd., London.
Distributed in Latin America by Kaiman & Polon,
Inc., New York City; in Australasia by Book & Film Services,
Artarmon, N.S.W., Australia; in India by UBS Publishers'
Distributors Pvt., Ltd., Delhi; in Japan by John Weatherhill, Inc.,
Tokyo.

For my family, with my love

Contents

Acknowledgments

An opportunity rarely arises for a student to thank his teachers publicly. I wish first to thank two men in particular: William G. Waite, for the encouragement and enlightenment he provided during my undergraduate years; and Allen Forte, whose tutelage, patience, and kindly supervision have made it possible for me to write this book.

Secondly, I would like to mention those courageous persons who have withstood—in shifts—the onslaught of my theoretical ravings while this study was in preparation. I thank them for their suggestions, their fortitude, and their humor: David Beach, Tom Fay, Andrew Fichter, Chris Hasty, Jon Kramer, Robert Morris, and Quentin Quereau.

Finally, it should be pointed out that several newly minted ideas in this study owe their existence to ones of an older coinage. In this I am particularly indebted to the theoretical work of Heinrich Schenker.

1

Historical Introduction

Any theory of rhythm can be only as valuable as the questions it seeks to answer. To evaluate past theories of rhythm is not merely to assess past solutions, but more significantly, it is to consider critically the scope of past inquiries and the methods by which the problems have been posed. Since the present study is concerned with the exploration of new theory, and since it is a response to what previously has been given for the theory of rhythm, it is necessary first to characterize former theories in light of their assumptions, methodologies, and applications.

In the broadest sense, the theory of musical rhythm has always been concerned with the elucidation of musical motion—motion that is differentiated by the durational value, pitch, or intensity of sounds but which, at the same time, presumably exhibits certain regularities. Yet at various moments in history, musicians have been confronted with issues of narrower and more immediate concern; for example, the scope of the theory of Aristoxenus (c. 350 B.C.) was limited, since it had only Greek musical culture as its subject.

Although the relationship of musical rhythm to the rhythm of poetic texts was not one of identity throughout Greek literature, Aristoxenan theory considered the organizations of music and artfully impassioned speech to be subject to the same general principles. The two were seen to differ only in the sense that music moved in specific pitch intervals, while speech blurred the distinctions between pitches.[1]

1. The relationships between the tonal, durational, and dynamic components of ancient Greek rhythm in music and language are complex and subject to varying interpretations. Warren Anderson summarizes the issue in his article "Word Accent and Melody in Ancient Greek Musical Texts," *Journal of Music Theory (JMT)* 17, no. 2 (1973): 186 ff.

"One may take as axiomatic the premise that differences in pitch primarily determined the accentual basis of Ancient Greek. This is a universally accepted fact, stated with great explicitness as early as the beginning of the Hellenistic period. Considered structurally, Greek bears notable resemblances to Sanskrit, which the Hindu grammarians always treated as a tone-accented language. It must have contained from the beginning an additional

A good Aristotelian, Aristoxenus had only to classify the different patterns into which poetic feet might be divided, according to genus and species, in order to answer to the question of musical rhythmic organization. He did this by depending upon a relative standard of motion—the *chronos protos*—which was the average length of a short syllable. A long syllable was then considered to be worth twice the durational value of a short one. With this quantitative model, the poetic foot was divided such that one of its components could be equal to, twice as long, or half again as long as another. Hence a rational system was devised that could account for rhythmic patterns in Greek music or poetry, but the vital link in the system was the closeness of the two arts with respect to the character of their rhythmic techniques.

The degree to which various other theories of rhythm have re-flected, like the one above, the prevailing musical style of their times is only one aspect of their history. Local trends in philo-sophical thinking and psychological theory have rendered a number of theories, if not obsolete, then at least benignly irrelevant to each other. To return to the above example, the system of Aristoxenus was already detached by two generations from Platonic theory—from which it differed. While Aristoxenus (and Aristotle) saw the emotive power, or *ethos*, of the Greek rhythmic modes as an important but auxiliary phenomenon, Plato had formerly considered that power as a more central problem that had to be resolved in order for rhythm to be properly understood.

Plato's reference to Damon of Athens[2] and to the ethos of the

element of stress. Eventually this replaced pitch as the basis of accentuation; when and how the change took place remains uncertain, but for the present inquiry such questions need not be resolved. A third factor, quantity, determined the nature of classical meters. In turn, the status of any given syllable as long (i.e., consisting of or containing a long vowel, a diphthong, or a short vowel followed by two consonants) or short (i.e., having a short vowel occurring either alone or followed by a single consonant) by normal rules might bear a necessary relation, either intrinsically or through its position, to the possibility of a given kind of accent occurring on that syllable. So far as musical settings are concerned, the horizontal dimension of syllable quantity clearly has to do above all with rhythmization. The exceptions, however, are worth specifying. A long syllable, especially when it occurs at a pause or during a moment of emotional crisis, may be set to more than one note. This practice was already well established by the early years of the 4th century B.C., when Plato complained about it."

2. Plato, *Republic* (III, 400), trans. F. Cornford (New York, 1959). "Next after the modes will come the principle governing rhythm, which will be, not to aim at a great variety of

rhythmic modes was couched in a wider body of speculation that considered the organization of the universe to reflect the order of music. Platonic music theory was further predicated on a special correspondence between musical motion and the motions of the soul, and as such it was inseparable from Platonic cosmology.[3] For Plato, the classification of the rhythmic modes had to be augmented by knowledge of the psychological effect of each individual pattern; even more significant was his wider curiosity about the mechanisms by which music variously affected the souls of men.[4] A modern equivalent of this latter kind of inquiry might fairly be called the psychology of musical perception.

I dwell on these ancient authors not only because of their obvious historical influence but, in addition, to show that since they asked different questions, two different theories of rhythm could coexist—even in a culture that was much more musically homogeneous than our own. One school could conceive of musical motion as a succession of syllabic modules and could be satisfied to classify the modules in accordance with a vocabulary of archetypal patterns (iambs, trochees, etc.). For the other school, the problem was more one of mental processes, and solutions were sought in the then-current theory of perception and in the context of vaster philosophical questions. The questions of one generation neither negated nor distorted the questions of the other but merely reflected different curiosities.

---

meters, but to discover the rhythms appropriate to a life of courage and self-control. . . . We shall consult Damon on this question, which meters are expressive of meanness, insolence, frenzy and the other such evils, and which rhythms we must retain to express their opposites."

3. Plato, *Timaeus* (90-d), trans. F. Cornford (New York, 1964). "The motions akin to the divine part in us are the thoughts and revolutions of the universe; these, therefore, every man should follow and, correcting those circuits in the head that were deranged at birth by learning to know the harmonies and revolutions of the world, he should bring the intelligent part, according to its pristine nature, into the likeness of that which intelligence discerns, and thereby win the fulfillment of the best life set by the Gods before mankind both for this present time and for the time to come."

4. Plato, *Republic* (III, 411), "When a man surrenders himself to music, allowing his soul to be flooded through the channels of his ears with those sweet and soft and mournful airs we spoke of, and gives up all his time to the delights of song and melody, then at first he tempers the high-spirited part of his nature, like iron whose brittle hardness is softened to make it serviceable; but if he persists in subduing it to such incantation, he will end by melting it away altogether."

Similarly, a theory written today need not absolutely refute its predecessors if it asks questions that others have not considered or if it is applicable to a style of music that others could not have known. The place where differences must almost invariably occur, however, is in the area of analysis, since a theory will regard its subject in terms of a delimited set of questions, and an analysis will reflect the character of the theory upon which it is based.

A theory of rhythm that views the structure of tonal music as a succession of chords, for example, will be accompanied by an analytic technique that is weighted towards evaluating the placement and rate of change of what it considers to be chords. Since the present study assumes that only some vertical events in tonal music are of paramount structural importance and that others serve a more rhetorical purpose, the weight of analysis will be thrown towards an elucidation of rhythmic structure that is characterized by levels of meaning. Such a structure will be referred to as a *rhythmic stratification*.

Before considering ancient theory any further it will be helpful to explore this last point. All general theories of rhythm which take durational length or dynamic intensity of sounds into account may be said to address themselves to the same phenomena. In the sense that duration is the length of time a signal is sounded and intensity is its loudness, duration and intensity have not changed historically in meaning. To the extent that pitch almost always relates to some system of pitch context, however, the historical view changes. New generations of theorists have altered the views of previous ones with respect to the structural functions of pitches as pitch theory has developed from modal, to tonal, to free-atonal, to serial systems; and this is not to mention the pitch relations that obtain in ethnographic spheres other than Euro-American.

Because of the manifest contingency that interpretations of rhythmic structure may have upon theories of pitch function, this study will take care to distinguish between the kinds of statements that proceed from *pitch to rhythm* and those that proceed from *rhythm to pitch*. A pitch-to-rhythm methodology is one that begins with some hierarchical theory of pitch such that, in the context of a composition, the rhythmic significance of a sound is indicated, led to, or believed caused by its pitch function. In contrast a rhythm-to-pitch decision is one that begins with some organized, purely rhythmic configuration and finds that, in the context of a composition, the pitch significance of a sound is indicated, led to, or believed caused by its rhythmic placement within that configuration.

This distinction between the two analytic procedures avoids a logical trap. Finding a pitch to be important because of its rhythmic placement and, at the same time, stipulating that the same rhythmic moment is important because an important pitch coincides with it is to reason in a circle. Keeping the two analytic approaches separate assures that the importance of a rhythmic moment will not both determine and be determined by the significance of a coinciding pitch event.

The first general rhythm-to-pitch approach to composition that we know about appeared in the twelfth century, and the extant theory that describes the system was written in the thirteenth. This can be found in the treatises of John of Garland, Jerome of Moravia, Anonymous IV, Odington, and the St. Emmeram Anonymous.[5] All of this literature comments on the modal rhythmic organization and notation of the music of the Notre Dame School.

The basis of modal rhythm was a system of six rhythmic modes, the product of a unique twelfth-century ratiocination. The modes were conceived of as patterns of ordered durational values, which patterns succeeded each other in time, and there is evidence that there is a more than passing relationship between these modes and earlier grammarians' models of poetic feet. They are presented here as they may appear as the smallest units of rhythm that are legal in the system; that is, two occurrences of the primary pattern of each rhythmic mode.

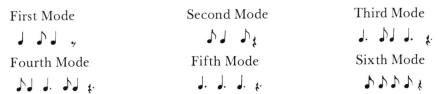

| First Mode | Second Mode | Third Mode |
| Fourth Mode | Fifth Mode | Sixth Mode |

5. "De Musica Mensurabili Positio," in E. de Coussemaker, *Scriptorum de Musica Medii Aevi* (Paris, 1864) (hereafter cited as CS), 1: 97 ff. Also CS 1: 175ff.; "Discantus Positio Vulgaris,' CS 1: 94 ff.; "De Mensuris et Discantu," CS 1: 327 ff.; "De Speculatione Musici," CS 1: 182 ff.; Heinrich Sowa, *Ein anonymer glossierter Mensuraltraktat 1279* (Konigsberg, 1930).

In *The Rhythm of Twelfth Century Polyphony*,[6] William Waite establishes the following concerning this subject:

1. Modal rhythm was quantitative and not qualitative. Pattern was determined solely by the durational length and the contextual placement of sounds and not by any present or felt dynamic stress. Moreover, although each mode was a function of ternary values, modal rhythm was not based on triple meter, nor for that matter on any concept of a system of grouped, equidistant accents.

2. The organization of music in accordance with fixed, temporal proportions was not an invention but a rediscovery made by the twelfth century. From the ninth century to the eleventh, music had been rhythmicized in terms of a notation that fixed a long and a short value, but the practice and notation had likely disappeared.

3. The reemergence of rhythm in the twelfth century was not accompanied by a reappearance of the old notation, and so in the absence of a system of notating fixed values the Notre Dame School originated a system by which ligatures were interpreted according to their notational context. This contextual notation obscures the true relationship that modal rhythm held to former treatises on metrics (i.e., studies of the organization of poetic feet in terms of syllables).[7]

6. William Waite, *The Rhythm of Twelfth Century Polyphony* (New Haven, 1954).

7. Two of Waite's most convincing arguments demonstrating this relationship are presented below:

"On the one side we find that a tradition of a metrical rhythm existed prior to the Notre Dame School and perhaps extended up to the appearance of modal rhythm. On the other side we find that theorists coming after the Notre Dame period speak of modes in terms related to metrics. Under such circumstances I believe the conclusion to be justifiable that the Notre Dame composers drew their modal rhythm from poetical feet" (ibid., p. 26).

"The composers were confronted with the problem of infusing rhythmically indifferent signs of notation with rhythmic significance. Their solution—modal notation—was a unique and entirely original one, having little or nothing in common with the previous rhythmic neumes. The originality of their solution is to be seen in three of the modes, the modii in *ultra mensuram*, which have no true, exact counterpart either in metrics or Gregorian rhythm, but which in their terminology and disposition reveal a certain affinity with the metrical system. It will later be demonstrated that these modes arose because of certain difficulties inherent in a notation which has no symbol for longa and brevis values. Because of these difficulties the third mode, which corresponds to the dactyl, came to have the rhythm ♩· ♪♩ instead of the proper metrical measurement ♩ ♪♪♩ . Despite the fact that the last note of the modal pattern is actually a longa recta containing two tempora, it is always referred to as a *brevis altera* (another kind of brevis, or a changed brevis).

4. The historical link between the rhythmic modes and metrics is likely to have been St. Augustine, whose influential *De Musica* (fourth century A.D.) was about musical rhythm.

5. Augustinian theory recognized a long value worth twice the short, the latter not unlike the earlier Greek chronos protos; but Augustine distinguished between syllable length in language and durational length in music. Musical rhythm was not merely the infinite repetition of a pattern but had limited measure. For example, whereas the strictness of rhythm was relaxed at the end of a line of poetry, the end of a musical line required a rest having a value equal to the remainder of the metric pattern. Hence different poetic meters following each other in a musical piece could retain the intelligibility of their patterns by suffering neither elongation nor abbreviation at end points.

The rhythm-to-pitch nature of compositions based on modal rhythm grows out of the character of the system. For any piece that was to be written one had first to choose one or more of the rhythmic modes. The rule was that the placement of vertical, consonant intervals generally occurred at initial points of the modal pattern in *organum purum* and at initial points of two or three simultaneously sounded modal units in compositions with many voices—and less frequently at intermediate points within modal patterns.[8]

It might be argued that twelfth-century polyphony equally may be said to have proceeded from pitch to rhythm. After all, was not each new repetition of modal pattern signalled by the presence of a vertical consonance? In fact, this was not the case. Since each modal pattern was predetermined by the theoretical system, its repetition was recognizable independently of pitch significance, even if coin-

Such a discrepancy in terminology could have arisen only if this note were considered to be the final short of a dactylic foot. If the modal system had been created without any reference to the metrical system, there would have been no need for this curious nomenclature: the brevis altera would simply have been called a long recta. But the fact remains that it is indeed called a brevis and so we must conclude that in theory the pattern of the third mode is equivalent to the dactyl foot" (ibid., pp. 28–29).

8. See Raymond F. Erikson's "Melodic Structure in Organum Purum: A Computer Assisted Study" (Diss., Yale University, 1970), for a closer discussion of these rules. His study of samples of *organum purum* indicates that "approximately 2 out of every 3 notes tested is [sic] a perfect consonance" (p. 66).

ciding points of repetition of pattern in more than one voice did not always form a consonance.[9] In addition, a methodology that determines rhythm in terms of pitch requires an accommodating pitch theory. The pitch theory of the period dealt with pitch modes, however, and these related mostly to beginnings, endings, and ranges of single voices. Beyond the classification of consonances and dissonances, this theory had nothing to say about overarching structures of pitch relating to voices in combination. In terms of the placement of vertical consonance when it did occur, and because of the severely limited domain of approved rhythmic patterns, it may then be said that in the twelfth century a rigorous system of rhythm determined pitch placement, perhaps more clearly than in any other time.

The twelfth-century system of rhythm is an important model because it so clearly subordinates any long-range relationships of pitch in compositions to the exigencies of rhythmic practice. In light of this it makes perfect sense to conceive of the rhythmic patterns of this period as a kind of stilted speech, proceeding in carefully proportioned units of poetic feet. An analysis might reasonably treat the rhythm of a melodic fragment of this period as it would that of a single line of measured talk. Even where the music presents a polyphonic texture, a thing rarely found in the performance of poetry without music, the ternary nature of all the rhythmic modes provides a coherent standard to which all voices must conform and in accordance with which all voices are aligned.

What is more, the rhythmic patterns of the literature were not complicated by dynamic stress but were determined solely by the quantity of time allotted to each sound, and so the analogy of musical motion to the rhythm of a single line of language (which is very much in accord with the dictum of Aristoxenus) need not have been compromised by the superimposition of levels of motion determined by pitch or intensity. But with the development of more complex systems of pitch, patterns determined by dynamic stress, and thicker musical textures there is reason to question whether this analogy of musical rhythm to the rhythm of language remains fruitful.

9. Erikson attests to this in his study. "Anon. IV clearly allows that the consonance rule is not the only one to be observed in composition: 'sometimes there are many longs by reason of the color and beauty of the melody, whether they will form concords or not, which reveal themselves in performance'" (p. 68).

The problem comes into clearer focus in the conceptual and notational systems of rhythm that developed during the late thirteenth century and the Renaissance. The purposes of this study can be served by a bare outline of these systems, since it is not the history of rhythmic practices or of systems of notation but rather an examination of theoretical concepts of temporal organization that is of present concern.

Where twelfth-century rhythm was notated in ligatures, the systems of the late thirteenth and fourteenth centuries developed specific graphic symbols for durational values: the long, breve, semibreve, minim, and so forth. In addition, fourteenth-century practice established a (roughly) standard rate of motion linked to the value of the breve—the *tempus*. Such development of systems of notation that indicated real time and not proportional duration may be said to have culminated in the *Ars Nova* of Philippe de Vitry (1291–1361). Where modal theory dealt with successions of patterns that could contain sounds of unequal durational values, the *Ars Nova* posited an external framework of relationships based on grouped, regular successions of equal time values, or meters.

As an architecture of levels of motion, this framework has evolved into the system of meters that enjoys current use. For the older system, as it developed, each notated value could be worth two or three of the next smaller notatable value; a tripartite division of the breve, for example, was indicated by the term *tempus perfectum* and a bipartite division by the term *tempus imperfectum*. Similarly the semibreves could be worth three minims (major prolation) or two (minor prolation). The breve itself could be contained three times (*modus perfectus*) or two times (*modus imperfectus*) by each long. By specifying modus, tempus, and prolation, then a composition established a system of abstract, logical interrelationships with respect to the organization of time.

This interrelationship of levels of motion may be viewed equally well in any of three ways, as if through one of the facets of a prism. One can consider, for instance, tempus perfectum and minor prolation as a relationship linked to the durational values of notes. In this case, each semibreve has a durational value equal to one-third the durational value of the breve—one-third of one tempus; and each minim has a durational value equal to half a semibreve, or one-sixth of a breve. This *duration relationship* characterized the notational systems of the Renaissance such that a change of tempus or prolation within a composition could mean assigning different durational values to symbols that remained unchanged on the page. Similarly, the Renaissance system of proportions made it possible to specify in a score that a graphic symbol be worth virtually any fraction or multiple of its former durational value. Modern notation can readily accomplish the same effect with groupettes, as for example the introduction of triplets in duple time.

A view through a second facet reveals these same relationships in terms of levels of motion. The semibreves succeed each other at three times the rate of succession of the breves, the minims at twice that of the semibreves and six times that of the breves. This *tempo relationship* could function to alter rates of motion[10] within a Renaissance composition in the absence of the metronome instructions that operate today. It should be stressed that this view is useful in characterizing a musical texture as one that exhibits simultaneously occurring, different rates of motion. This aspect of musical rhythm may be made more apparent in Renaissance music because simultaneous but different rates of motion are often specified separately in notation as multiple meters, whereas the notation of later music tends to subsume alternate levels of motion under the domain of a single meter.

The third view is more metaphorical in that its image of the above relationships is static. Each breve specifies a length of time, like a written line of specific length, which is divided into three parts by the location of the semibreves and into six parts by the location of the minims. This model, based on the *division* of equal units of time, is employed in current notation. The measure, flanked by bar lines, is seen as a unit of time that is conceptually segmented according to the time signature; and in certain well-known styles of music, the measures themselves conceptually divide the durations of entire compositions into equal segments.

Whether viewed in terms of duration, tempo, or time-division, the framework of logical relationships like those described above must be seen preeminently as a conceptual technology whose object is to

---

10. "Rates of motion" should not be confused with the then-accepted standard of motion, the *tactus*, which was likely unaffected by notation.

prescribe the accurate real time performance of music. Indeed, the rift between the technology itself and the aesthetic patterns it may be used to specify is as wide as that between a Cartesian grid and the linear shapes that may be drawn on it. The special irony of the musical system is that the technology which makes a multiplicity of rhythmic designs graphically possible is not adequate by itself to describe the aesthetic function and compositional coherence of those same designs.

Later Renaissance theory did make tentative comment about relationships between pitch and rhythm. Zarlino, for example, stressed the stylistic rule that a sequence of four semiminims could form dissonances with another slower-moving voice on the second and fourth notes but had to form consonances on the first and third. Yet just as easily, Vincenzo Galilei could mitigate the severity of this rule with his approval of a consonance on the first note and a dissonance on each of the remaining three.[11] In short, the theory of rhythm of the fourteenth century and the Renaissance was mostly a theory relating to notation and to abstract rates of motion with little rigorously consistent comment as regards the formation of and the relationships between rhythmic designs as aesthetic objects.[12]

Virtually until the eighteenth century, the two broad models that have been discussed here constituted the theory of rhythm. The first model took its inspiration from Greek systems of organizing syllabic patterns of spoken language, and its application to twelfth-century rhythm hangs on the intimacy between rhythmic modal patterns and the metrical patterns of poetry. The applicability of this first system to freer rhythmic designs, however, is subject to question because its original form merely classified syllabic patterns but shed little light on the relationship those patterns might have to any pitch

11. For a discussion of this and others of Galilei's and Zarlino's differences see Claude V. Palisca's "Vincenzo Galilei's Counterpoint Treatise: A Code for the Secunda Pratica," *Journal of the American Musicological Society (JAMS)* 9, no. 2 (1958): 81 ff.

12. A notable exception is the fourteenth-century practice of isorhythm. Here a sequence of pitches is varied while an ever-repeating configuration of time values remains unchanged. I have not included isorhythm as a theory of rhythm per se because it is not general, even in terms of the music of its own period, but characterizes only one particular compositional technique. (Nevertheless, in the context of a composition that employs it, an isorhythm makes an admirable structure with which to describe rhythmic coherence.) Similarly, later discussions of the rhythm of various dance forms are basically descriptive and are not, in themselves, theories of rhythm.

structures that generate them. Even more problematic is the validity of the vocabulary of archetypes that makes up the classification. It is not clear what puts the limit on this vocabulary. A theoretical basis for determining a finite number of primary rhythmic patterns such that any other design must be an aggregate of two or more of these patterns has never been adequately specified.

The second model derives from the mensural theory of Philippe de Vitry. Since the development of that system, it has been known to music theory that individual compositions may be rhythmically structured according to hierarchies. These hierarchies organize different rates of musical motion in that they specify a relationship between a succession of durations of a given value and a succession of durations that augment or diminish that value, usually by some multiple of two or three. But though the mensuration of note values has served as the logical framework of rhythmic hierarchies in the abstract and notational sense, its language alone cannot sufficiently describe the way varying rates of the occurrences of events are manipulated aesthetically in a composition.

During the eighteenth century the theory of rhythm took a departure from the study of syllabic models and systems of notation and became directed towards the study of form as it relates to rhythm. Here a distinction must be made between the explicit and the implicit theory of the period. Terms borrowed from the punctuation of language (period, colon, semicolon) did enjoy usage, and theorists of the period did explicitly describe the shape of melodic lines as the they would parse sentences.[13] At the same time, however, a development of analytic concepts of pitch structure led to principles of understanding musical motion that reflect an implicit tendency towards pitch-to-rhythm methodology.

An early example of this kind of thinking may be found in Johann David Heinichen's *Der General-Bass in der Composition.*[14] In a section on two- and three-voiced arpeggios, Heinichen illustrates the notion that some pitch structures are not simply linear successions

13. Johann Mattheson does this in *Der vollkommene Capellmeister* (Hamburg, 1739). A good summary of Mattheson's use of grammatical and rhetorical terms to describe music can be found in Hans Lennenberg's "Johann Mattheson on Affect and Rhetoric in Music (II)," *JMT* 2, no. 2 (1958): 193 ff.

14. Dresden, 1728.

from note to note but are, rather, vertical structures of which the separate voices are displaced in time (example 1.1).[15]

Example 1.1

The two voices in example 1.1, A are joined in a compound line as illustrated in example 1.1, B. The implicit meaning of the equivalence of A to B for the theory of rhythm becomes clear if the process is reversed and one considers A as an analysis of B. This would imply that the sixteenth-note passages contain a stratum of motion in eighth-notes—as indicated by example 1.1, A. Since such a determination is made on the basis of the pitch placement and contour of the two voices, it can be inferred that the separation of the patterns of example 1.1, B into the rhythmic levels shown in example 1.1, A is made on the basis of pitch-to-rhythm.

This example adumbrates a body of later theory that was based on the same principle; i.e., that levels of motion could now be found in music on the basis of pitch interpretation. Kirnberger, for example, indicated that a musical phrase could be divided into segments of one size or another by points of arrival at cadences. In 1777 he defined rhythm as follows:

> One uses this word in two ways. Sometimes it means what the ancients called *Rhythmoponie*, that is the rhythmic character of a piece; but on the other hand it means a phrase [*Satz*] or segment [*Einschnitt*]. It is used in the first meaning when one says, "This composition is in an incorrect Rhythmus" or "(It) has no good Rhythmus." In the other meaning one uses it when he says "a Rhythmus (*Einschnitt*) of 4 measures."[16]

15. The example is taken from p. 558 of Heinichen's study.

16. Trans. David Beach from Kirnberger's *Die Kunst des reinen Satzes in der Musik* (Berlin, 1777). vol. 1, part 2, chap. 4, p. 137.

A basis for this definition may be found in an intriguing study made by Joseph Riepel, whose *Anfangsgründe zur musikalischen Setz-kunst*[17] possibly influenced Kirnberger's later thinking.

Riepel's treatise is written in the traditional form of a dialogue between a callow Discantor and his Praeceptor. In chapter one, "Von der Taktordnung," the Praeceptor considers a minuet that the student has written (example 1.2).[18]

Example 1.2

He immediately launches into a critique of the piece, which is not an analysis of its harmonic or contrapuntal implications but rather a commentary directed purely toward the formation and the manipulation of rhythmic groups in an aesthetic sense. In the course of improvement, the piece takes an alternate form, illustrated in example 1.3.

17. Regensburg, 1754.

18. This and subsequent musical examples presented by Riepel are from p. 2 ff. of his book. A fuller historical discussion of Riepel's ideas may be found in Arnold Feil's dissertation, "Satztechnische Fragen in den Kompositionslehren von F. E. Niedt, J. Riepel und H. Chr. Koch," (Heidelberg, 1955).

Example 1.3

Riepel has clearly concentrated on the rhythmic reorganization of the piece by shortening the second section to 8 bars and altering note patterns to make them rhythmically more homogeneous. A discussion of pattern in chapter two will consider this aspect of Riepel's minuet more closely, but here the unstated principles of pitch levels as they relate to rhythmic levels are more relevant.

In discussing the improvement of mm. 9–13 Riepel offers his student a variety of options. Here the sequence as the student has written it contains a segment of three bars followed by a segment of two bars (example 1.4).

Example 1.4

Riepel does not indicate how he arrives at this segmentation, but it is obvious that the content of bar 11 is grouped with the two preceding measures and that a similar bar does not appear after m. 13.

The first suggested alternative eliminates bar 11 (example 1.5, A). This implies for Riepel a bisection of the four bars into two "Zweier." I presume that he reaches this conclusion through a recognition that the harmony changes at bar 11 (pitch-to-rhythm) or that the pattern of notes (♩ ♫♩ ♩ ♩) repeats at that same point (rhythm-to-pitch). Other alternate versions of the same example, however, clearly depend more on pitch significance for their segmentation, since they do not contain a succession of identical rhythmic patterns that are each two measures long (example 1.5, B and C).

Example 1.5

It might be objected that Riepel is speaking of motivic form here and that the notion of rhythm in this kind of analysis is too closely linked to an idiomatic, eighteenth-century concept of "Rhythmus." This would be to ignore, however, that Riepel's concept of segmentation is based on the idea of division, and in light of what was established earlier in this chapter it may then be said that the same segmentation gives rise to a duration relationship and a tempo relationship. Thus to divide a phrase into two "Zweier" is to indicate that each segment has a time span of two measures, and it is also to say that this division creates a level of motion that proceeds at a corresponding rate. What appears first to be a question of motivic form thus appears also to be an equally compelling question of rhythmic levels.

Riepel's subsequent expansion of the phrase into two groups of three bars ("Dreier") illustrates this and suggests that some concept of pitch prolongation informs the segmentation (example 1.6, A and B).

Example 1.6

In comparing the first segments of these examples with those of example 1.5, B they each are seen to contain an added third measure, which Riepel indicates to be logically attached to their respective segments rather than being the beginnings of new segments. The reason for this might well be asked.

Since Riepel does not extensively discuss his theoretical principles apart from their practical applications I will have to proceed by inference here. One reason may be that the motion within the second bars in examples 1.6, A and B does not resolve to an *a* but rather passes through that pitch into the third bar; or, to put it another way, this motion prolongs the *b-flat* and the dominant harmony of F for an additional measure. Where example 1.5, B makes a small close on an *a* in its second measure, examples 1.6, A and B employ the *a* as a passing tone—filling in the consonant third between *b-flat* and *g* (*g* is implied in example 1.6, B)—so that the close in the third bar leads from *g* to *f* in an inner voice. A similar process occurs in the fifth and sixth bars of these examples.[19]

Riepel's unstated principle of judgment here must have been his impression that the phrase is divided into two segments by only a final arrival on *a* and/or *f* and not by a passing use of those tones. The level of motion (2 groups of three bars) represented by example 1.6, then, depends upon a recognition that the third and sixth bars are of equivalent structural significance and that any motion separating these equivalent pitch events occurs on another level. That Riepel understood this principle of prolongation is clearly demonstrated by his further expansion of the phrase into two groups of 4 bars each ("Vierer"), shown in example 1.7.

Example 1.7

19. I anticipate objection to my reading of example 1.6, A as a prolongation of *b-flat* which resolves to *a* only on the last beat of m. 3. In this and subsequent discussions of Riepel's examples I am treating them in terms of their being self-sufficient and written

Here the *a* in the second bar unquestionably passes from *g* to *b-flat*, prolonging the *b-flat*, while the *a* in the fourth bar is an arrival from *b-flat* and is equivalent in significance to the *b* in bar 8.

Riepel's examples resonate with implications for the theory of rhythm. The idea that a rhythmic level may be determined by a level of pitch significance is provocative in itself, but it is especially dramatized in these examples because they are unaccompanied melodic lines; other levels of rhythm must be contained within them rather than in some accompanying part. By dividing such melodic lines into measured segments by pitch criteria, the theorists of the eighteenth century provided a basis for concepts that had not been formerly accessible, even though they never explicitly stated those concepts.

First, they implied that though a melody may appear to be a single succession of pitches, these pitches may be assigned hierarchies according to function. On the basis of such pitch hierarchies, melodies may then be divided into multiple voices and segments (or they may be described as summations of multiple voices and segments).

Second, these theorists suggested that the division of a melody into segments is one way to describe a rhythmic event, so the presence of organized motion on a level other than the immediate level of note succession is implied. Their study of these other levels of

---

for unaccompanied solo instruments. In these terms, the *a* in m. 2 of example 1. 6, B is a much more convincing illustration of a note that has a passing function.

Yet 1. 6, A must be seen as altering 1. 6, B only to the extent that the *a* in the second bar is given more time. Underlying each of these passages is the first note—*c*—which acts as a bass and must be considered operative until it ascends to *f* in the final measure. Thus a reading of both passages must be shown as follows:

Saying that the reductive sketches of both passages are effectively identical does not imply, however, that their rhythmic differences are insignificant. Quite to the contrary, the rhythmic character of either passage is determined to a great extent by the presence of the passing *a* on either the second or third beat of m. 2. This is a pitch-to-rhythm statement, and interestingly, the reverse does not apply; it would not be equally correct to say that the function of the *a* is determined by its duration. This is because the note is enclosed by and connects two members of the dominant harmony regardless of its durational value.

motion had to have rested, in part, on a pitch-to-rhythm methodology.

Finally, eighteenth-century investigations of this aspect of rhythm appear to have served a new curiosity about the aesthetic principles of rhythm as they apply to uniquely musical structures and not an interest in the theory of notation or the theory of poetic versification. To see this difference, one need only compare the kind of stratification of a single melodic line that is implied in Riepel's treatise with an alternate interpretation that would view the melody as if it were a succession of stressed and unstressed syllables (or with an interpretation that would segment the melody in terms of rhythmic notation alone). The implication of Riepel's models is that there are uniquely musical principles that mediate between the pitches and the rhythmic configurations.

The major treatises of the nineteenth century did not continue to investigate rhythm in the context of pitch function, but rather separated issues of the theory of rhythm from the considerable controversies that arose over the nature of tonal pitch systems. Questions pertaining to the derivation and use of harmonic structures, the origin of the minor triad, and the theoretical explanations of the nature of consonance were problematic subjects that would have beclouded any attempt to base a theory of rhythm on a rigorous theoretical system of pitch relations. Thus nineteenth-century theorists were concerned with rhythm as a self-enclosed system of organizing time, and in this context they introduced a rigor that was previously lacking in the theory of rhythm.[20]

The ideas of Moritz Hauptmann, Hugo Riemann, and Rudolph Westphal are important in this respect. Westphal's system was derivative, as may be seen by the title of his major work, *Allgemeine Theorie der musikalischen Rhythmik seit J. S. Bach auf Grundlage der Antiken*.[21] This treatise resuscitated the chronos protos along with Aristoxenan metrics and applied the ancient thought to Western art music. Since this tendency has reappeared in the twentieth

20. For a description of nineteenth-century theories of rhythm, see Carl Alette, "Theories of Rhythm" (Diss., Eastman School of Music, 1951), and Howard Elbert Smither, "Theories of Rhythm in the Nineteenth and Twentieth Centuries . . ." (Diss., Cornell University, 1960).

21. Leipzig, 1880.

century it will be better to delay a discussion of its merits until a
later section of this chapter.

The most influential theory of the period was written by Moritz
Hauptmann and Hugo Riemann, with the latter acknowledging his
debt to the former. Hauptmann's ideas have often been rejected
because of some somewhat arbitrary use of Hegelian philosophy,[22]
but it should be pointed out that he had a great deal to do with
introducing the idea that music theory be put on a logical and
systematic footing. In *The Nature of Harmony and Meter*[23] he
separated his kind of music theory from former models.

> We must distinguish this manner of theoretical interpretation from the
> theory which bears immediately upon practice: the theory of harmonic
> and metrical shape in itself apart from the theory of the art of composi-
> tion [p. xlvi].

He then suggested that the principles of this more general theory
have to comply with broader, logical concepts, and for his own
system he appropriated the dialectical logic of Hegel. As such,
Hauptmann's section on meter is the first attempt to elucidate the
organization of motion *sui generis*—an attempt to uncover what lies
at the base of purely formal relationships between alternate divisions
of a time span. A short summary of his ideas follows.

1. A theory of rhythm must be universal and general but applicable
to each specific case.

2. The ultimate ground for universal musical principles is an
innate, human predisposition to their logical form (i.e., the dialectic). "That which is musically inadmissible is not so because it is
against a rule determined by musicians but because it is against a
natural law given to musicians from mankind, because it is logically
untrue and of inward contradiction" (p. xl).

3. Meter refers to equal time division, rhythm to unequal time
division. Musical rhythm is inconceivable without meter since it
"derives its meaning" from meter.

4. The presence of rhythm and meter is contingent upon an arrangement of accented and unaccented elements.[24]

---

22. Smither's evaluation tends to concentrate on this weakness. It is likely that Hauptmann is not read as much as he might be nowadays because of his abstruse Hegelian streak.

23. Trans. W. E. Heathcote (London, 1888). The original German edition appeared in
1864.

24. "No accent can be an isolated determination nor occur in a single portion of time as a

5. The basic metrical form is duple time, a unit of time followed by another equal to itself. Hauptmann here considers motion in terms of the duration between beats rather than the moments of attack of the beats themselves. Hence two units of time are defined by two beats with a continuing beat implied.[25]

6. Accent is a logically determined phenomenon that arises out of the beginning of a sequence of events. Thus in duple division the first unit of time determines the second and is therefore accented.

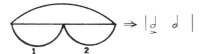

Since the point of beginning of a recurring sequence can logically be placed within the sequence as well, however, Hauptmann explains the upbeat as that which precedes a displaced beginning.

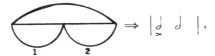

but:

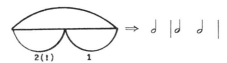

7. Triple time is the antithesis of duple. Hauptmann diagrams it as an intersection of two units of duple time.

---

solitary element not standing in an arrangement of accents and not in reciprocal relation with all the other parts of time in a metrical unity" (Hauptmann, p. 253).

25. This and the following drawings are based on Hauptmann's diagrams.

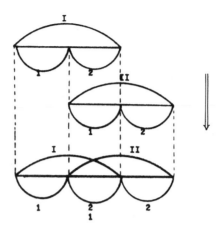

The first large duple unit (I) is followed by a second (II), which inter-
sects with the first as shown in the above diagram. Further, each of
the constituent duple units has a first and second component. Hauptmann then determines an accentual scheme based on the interrelationship between the two large duple units and the components of
their own bisections.

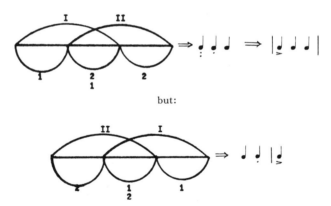

Hence the point where there is the most overlapping of beginnings
of sequences (1s) become the downbeat.

8. Quadruple time becomes the Hegelian synthesis of duple and
triple; it is made up of the intersection of two triple units.

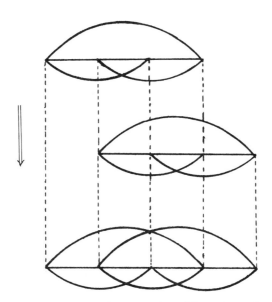

Since it is the product of an intersection (like triple time) but consists of two equal parts (like duple time), quadruple time is seen to mediate the opposition of the other two. Hauptmann explains any other divisions of time (5s, 6s, 7s) as either compound meters or some summation of duple and triple time.

9. Hauptmann then applies the same methodology to rhythmic forms; i.e., unequal time divisions, and shows them to be based on metrical schemes.

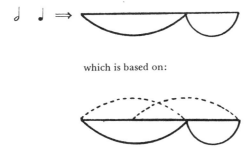

which is based on:

10. In a highly significant chapter on speech meter, Hauptmann points out that the traditional symbols for long and short (-,⌣) syllables are far inferior to music notation for the depiction of rhythm.

> The customary way of marking verse meter is wanting in means to dis-
> criminate accurately the fine shades of rhythm. Nor is it employed to
> disclose the inner metrical structure of verses. By the scheme which it
> presents we are taught only the order of succession of long and short
> syllables which taken by itself, is but the surface, the outside of the
> edifice of verse [p. 307].

Of the above set of ideas, Hauptmann's contribution would have
been sufficient if the most he had accomplished by his treatise was to
convince a generation of music theorists that an all-inclusive system
based on logical principles is the most desirable kind of theory. Indeed this was accomplished, as evidenced by Riemann's later statement:

> If one asks what the task of a theory of art really consists of the answer
> can only be that it is to establish the natural principles that govern the
> artistic work, unconsciously or consciously, and to set them forth in a
> system of logically related precepts.[26]

The bulk of Riemann's theory of rhythm is written in his *Musikalische Dynamik und Agogik* (Hamburg, 1884) and *System der
musikalischen Rhythmik und Metrik* (Leipzig, 1903). The former
work explicates his seminal idea—that rhythm is determined by
accents of dynamic shading and accents arising out of a minuscule
lengthening of durational values at points of segmentation within
motives (agogic).[27]

Riemann owed a debt to Hauptmann even when he disagreed with
him. For example, his logical model of a rhythmic system differs
from Hauptmann's, but it employs the dialectic. This time, though,
an undifferentiated duration is the thesis, a divided one is the antithesis, and groupings within the division form the synthesis.

26. Trans. Allen Forte from *Geschichte Der Musiktheorie...*(Leipzig, 1898), chap. 10,
p. 450: "Fragt man worin eigentlich die Aufgabe der Theorie einer Kunst bestehe, so kann
die Antwort nur lauten, dass die dieselbe die natürlich Gesetzmassigkeit welche das Kunst-
schaffen bewusst oder unbewusst regelt, zu ergrunden und in einem System logisch zussa-
menhangender Lehrsatz darzugelegen habe."
27. "As the essence of the harmonic-melodic element is change of pitch, so the essence
of the metric-rhythmic element is change of living energy; of *tone-intensity* (dynamics) on
the one hand, and of *rapidity of tone succession* (agogics, tempo) on the other." Carl Alette,
op. cit. Translated from Riemann's *Musikalische Dynamik und Agogic*, p. 10: "Wie das
Wesen des Harmonisch-Melodischen die Veränderung der Tonhöhe ist, so ist das Wesen des
Metrisch-Rhythmischen die Veränderung der lebendigen Kraft, einerseits der Tonstärke
(*Dynamik*) anderseits der Geschwindigkeit der Tonfolge (*Agogic, Tempo*)."

Thesis: _____

Antithesis: _

Synthesis: ⌣ ⌣ ⌣ ⌣ ⌣ ⌣ ⌣ ⌣ ⌣ ⌣ ⌣ ⌣ ⌣ ⌣ ⌣ -

Both of his books are directed specifically towards the study of phrasing motives, however, and where Hauptmann uses no musical examples Riemann's work abounds in them. The following should be taken as no more than an outline of his ideas.

1. The concept of metrical accent is similar to Hauptmann's, except that Riemann simplified the possible kinds of accentual schemes down to three classes:

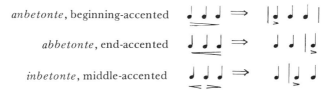

anbetonte, beginning-accented

abbetonte, end-accented

inbetonte, middle-accented

2. Of the above schemes, Riemann considered that the first is fallacious. He reasoned that all music employs an upbeat; either an upbeat is implied before a composition that appears to begin on a downbeat, or such a piece begins with a downbeat but immediately gives rise to an upbeat scheme. For example, the trochaic pattern of versification is always transformed, according to him, into an iambic one:

It should be mentioned that this is dead wrong, and Riemann's intellectual parochialism in this respect led to his distorted view of the twelfth-century second rhythmic mode as the first mode with an upbeat .[28]

28. "In a succession of tones that consistently alternates between longs and shorts (iambic or trochaic): , the longs are clearly emphasized by their value so that they become the carriers of the rhythm, while the shorts only repeatedly execute the connection from one beat to the next in succession. The long is thus the main beat, the heavier, the more important; the short is an adjacent beat and appears weak opposite the long. Our notation expresses this through the metric orderings: or " (my translation, from Riemann's *System ...*, p. 9).

3. Another of Riemann's prejudices was his belief that long-span rhythmic structures have an ideal length based on some multiple of the number four. His reason was based on the visual analogy of symmetry and on Hauptmann's view that an ideal structure is made up of an element that is followed by another equal to itself. Hence a basic two-bar motive (1+1) is followed by another, and these four bars are balanced by another four in sequence.

4. Despite this, Riemann believed that divisions of time into groups of fives and sevens are logical primitives and not aggregates of duple and triple divisions as suggested by Hauptmann.

5. Riemann also introduced the idea of the rhythmic resultant. This is the vertical summation of any simultaneously sounding rhythmic patterns.

6. Alternate levels of motion within metrical schemes (e.g., triplets in duple time) were considered by him to be not new meters but rather tied subdivisions of the beat.

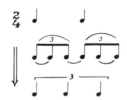

7. Riemann viewed the ultimate task of the theory of rhythm to be the determination of accentual patterns and the correct interpretation of phrase divisions in music. Significantly, he stated in chapter 10 of *Musikalische Dynamik und Agogik* that he used the word "phrase" where former theorists used the word "Rhythmus" (cf. Kirnberger).

8. In the musical examples of *System der musikalischen Rhythmik und Metrik* there is some consideration of pitch significance, but not

enough by which to derive any consistent method. As Smithers
points out in his dissertation (p. 236),

> Occasionally he takes into consideration harmonic and other aspects of
> texture . . . but for the large majority of his analyses he presents only one
> motive structure as an illustration of a certain type without presenting
> reasons for his particular motivic interpretation.

By the twentieth century, then, the theory of rhythm had gained
another model for its formation. To syllabic models, theories of
notation, and implicit eighteenth-century concepts of aesthetic
designs as they relate to pitch, the nineteenth century contributed
alternative, self-enclosed logical models.

To complete the picture of what is available to the present age, one
must mention psychology. This last kind of theory has never been
systematically formulated by any music theorist, but rather it supplies a bank of common data for use by all theorists. In general, it
is any theory of perception that attempts to explain how rhythmic
organization originates, psychologically or psycho-physiologically,
in the human organism and how the organism perceives and responds
to organized motion.

Reflecting the many models of psychology itself, this kind of study
may cling tightly to a physiological model based on either internal
biological rhythms (heartbeat, pulse, alpha waves, and other internal
clocks) or on external motions (walking, skipping, riding a horse,
etc.). A gestalt-oriented approach seeks to uncover the intrinsic
operations or constructions of perception, such as the presumably
innate, human tendency to group a series of steady pulses into recurrent cells of two or three pulses each.

To the extent that research in this area is concerned with cerebral
mechanisms, it reflects the curiosity of Plato more than that of
Aristoxenus, and although much interesting information may be
gained from such study, the following question should be asked:
if it were possible to trace every musical phenomenon across every
neural synapse in the brain, or if it were possible to predict a psychological response to every musical phenomenon, would this information tells us anything about the way aesthetic designs are uniquely
combined in individual compositions—or would it reveal the musical
principles by which different rhythmic designs originate and are

related to each other in a coherent system? Quite to the contrary, it is more likely that a musical theory aimed at uncovering the principles by which rhythm can be uniquely differentiated in an aesthetically coherent composition would prove an invaluable aid to a psychologist, who must first understand the true nature of what is to be perceived before he can construct a theory of perception.

This issue, along with others, is pointed up in an eclectic work written recently: Cooper's and Meyer's *The Rhythmic Structure of Music*.[29] Although the authors do not credit the sources of many of their ideas, it is clear that they rely on psychological research, Aristoxenan metrics and its nineteenth-century counterparts, and the works of Hauptmann and Riemann. Nevertheless they evidently overlooked the eighteenth-century theorists. To make the statement "There are many textbooks on harmony and counterpoint but none on rhythm" (p. v) is to ignore Riepel's work entirely.

Cooper and Meyer lean most heavily on a theory of accents that is based on the analogy to linguistic versification. As I have stressed before, the ultimate problem of such a methodology (Westphal's as well as Cooper's and Meyer's) arises when one tries to limit the vocabulary of archetypes to a finite number of primitives such that other patterns are aggregates of members of the vocabulary. *The Rhythmic Structure of Music* posits a vocabulary of five patterns:

iamb	∪ –
anapest	∪ ∪ –
trochee	– ∪
dactyl	– ∪ ∪
amphibrach	∪ – ∪

These are considered to be the five basic ways of producing rhythm; i.e., of combining strong and weak beats. The patterns, of course, originate in Greek metrics, and the contingency of rhythm on strong and weak beats was fully explicated first by Hauptmann and then by Riemann. The trouble comes when Cooper and Meyer begin to account for alternate combinations:

Other possible combinations of strong and weak beats, such as ♩♩ ♩ ♪

29. Chicago, 1960.

or ♩ ♪ ♩ will be analyzed as combinations of the basic groups

given above, ♫ ♩ ♪ and ♩ ♪ ♩ [pp. 6–7].

This methodology implies two problems:

1. To say that ♫ ♩ ♪ is equivalent to ♫ ♩ ♪ is to

concentrate on the pattern of accentuation at the expense of warping

the unique time values of ♫ ♩ ♪ as a five-group by making

them resemble the conformation of a four-group (♪ ♩ ♪).

Although this looks suspiciously like Riemann's predilection for the
number four, it should be remembered that even he considered
groupings of odd numbers of beats to be logical primitives.

2. The second problem is more serious since it seems reasonable
to warp time values if one is more curious about general patterns of
accents than about real time. What is not reasonable, however, is to
fail to do this with consistency. Thus, for example, if one transforms

♫ ♩ ♪ into ♫ ♩ ♪ , the same may be done to the

anapest and to the dactyl,

♫ ♩ ⟹ ♫ ♩ ∥ ♩ ♫ ⟹ ♩ ♫

and this reduces the primary vocabulary by two patterns. Such a
reduction would make the system resemble Riemann's schematization of beginning, middle, and end-accented forms. In addition,
though, the authors' explanation of their second example ♩ ♪ ♩

may be applied equally to the amphibrach (♪ ♩ ♪) so that,

if their methodology were consistently and not arbitrarily applied,
there would be only iambs and trochees.

The problem is then one of criteria. Why is a reductive method
applicable to the universe of rhythmic designs but not to patterns
within the authors' primary vocabulary? One answer may be that
they consider the primary vocabulary to pertain to groups of two-

and three-syllable markings only. Echoing Hauptmann, then, other designs would be aggregates of patterns made up of twos and threes. An assumption that the mind tends to comprehend large patterns as aggregates of smaller units of two or three elements does indeed lend support to a highly-restricted, primary vocabulary of rhythm. But this assumed kind of mental grouping must be seen as a general psychological tendency—operative only under certain conditions. The possibility that the mind may operate in this way is not a law of perception.

Cooper and Meyer fail to understand this in their analysis of the "Dance of the Adolescents" from *The Rite of Spring* (example 1.8).

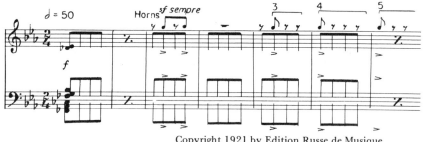

Example 1.8

They claim: "At the outset the metric organization, whether imposed by the mind of the listener or by the articulation of the orchestra, is clearly in duple meter. Nor is this impression weakened by the stressed offbeats in measure 3. Instead, these stresses, coming as dynamic intensifications frequently do, confirm our sense of duple meter" (p. 98).

There are some aspects of the music that their example and their statement ignore. First, their musical example overlooks the fact that, for "the articulation of the orchestra," the opening bars are played by strings, and the bowing indication specifically requires a down-bow on each eighth note—followed by the instruction *sempre simile*. Clearly, Stravinsky did not want the normal, up-bow and down-bow alternations to superimpose a duple grouping on the pattern. Furthermore, the dynamic marking is forte, and Stravinsky prescribes no shading within the measure.

Second, even assuming that the tendency to group in twos or threes operates "in the mind of the listener," this principle alone is not sufficient grounds for claiming that the grouping is duple in this example. In fact, a triple grouping is equally possible and would make the first stress in the third bar of the example fall on the assumed beat—an attractive but incorrect alternative.

The presence of duple grouping in this example may be postulated, however, not by the mind alone but by the one thing Cooper and Meyer do not consider: the compositional context. This passage is immediately preceded by the duple pitch alternations shown in example 1.9, and the momentum they establish may be thought of as extending into the bars that follow them. Hence a compositional context, and not a universal theoretical principle, may give rise to a duple interpretation in the mind of the listener, but the mind cannot act ex nihilo in this regard. It must first be informed by prior events in the composition.

Copyright 1921 by Edition Russe de Musique
Copyright assigned 1947 to Boosey & Hawkes, Inc.
Reprinted by permission

Example 1.9

Returning now to the original question, there is no law of perception that grounds Cooper's and Meyer's delimiting of five metric patterns (each containing two or three syllables) to the exclusion of any others, and if there is any basis for doing so, they do not discuss it.[30] The net result is a theory that arbitrarily calls some patterns

30. They refer the reader to James L. Mursell's *The Psychology of Music* (New York, 1937). Mursell considers the rhythm of music to be "the organization of its stresses, durations and pauses considered in abstraction from its tonal content" (p. 149). To support this abstraction, Mursell states: "Woodrow has ascertained that a periodic variation in pitch seems to have no rhythm-producing influence whatever" (p. 171)—an observation clearly refuted by Heinichen's arpeggios described in this study.

The source of the Cooper and Meyer vocabulary is found in chapter 5 of Mursell, where he describes their five metric patterns, plus the tribrach (u u u) and spondee (- -), as "the basic constituent elements of the whole structure of musical rhythm" (pp. 176–177). Neither does Mursell, however, enlarge upon the theoretical basis of this statement. He refers us instead to: Raymond B. Stetson, "Teaching of Rhythm," *Musical Quarterly* 9 (1923): 181–190; George Pullen Jackson, "The Rhythmic Forms of the German Folk

unique and others non-unique, for if the dactyl (– u u) is to be distinguished from the trochee (– u) then there is no reason to deprive the infinite variety of other unique patterns of its richness.[31] In addition, if the use of versification techniques is internally problematic it is also historically paradoxical. One need only juxtapose Moritz Hauptmann's use of music notation to analyze the cups and slashes of poetic rhythm with Cooper's and Meyer's use of verse notation to analyze notated, musical rhythm to have a true picture of ships passing in the night.

The images of rhythm that the above, former generations of theorists have bequeathed to the present may thus be characterized as varied and problematic. To summarize briefly:

1. Our notational system exhibits a genius for specifying virtually any conceivable free rhythmic design, but the notation of music is not necessarily its analysis.

2. Rhythmic designs are generally observed to be not simply patterns of pitches of specific durations, but they are also understood to be *interpreted* structures; i.e., they are shaped by the location of

---

Songs," *Modern Philology* 13 (1915–16): 561–581; 14 (1916–17): 65–92; 15 (1917–18): 79–102; and George H. Wedge, *Rhythm in Music: A Textbook* (New York, 1927). Yet, according to Mursell, none of these former accounts "seems wholly satisfactory taken alone" (p. 177). Cooper's and Meyer's restriction of the rhythmic vocabulary is thus based on a system which they attribute to Mursell, who never explained the basis of what he did but who refers us, instead, back to other writers who did not formulate the system satisfactorily in his opinion.

The earliest source that Mursell mentions, Jackson's article, is found in a journal of philology, and its subject matter is restricted to German folk songs. Here the truth comes out. Every one of Jackson's examples is an unaccompanied syllabic setting of a German text; the most melismatic activity to be found is the occasional addition of one extra note to a syllable. For this kind of musical rhythm Jackson finds a fruitful analogy in the rather limited structures of linguistic verse pattern, and indeed who would dare disagree? The difficulty of this schematization enters only when these authors platonize their metric patterns into ideal forms or types. By doing this, Mursell indicates "in actual rhythmic experience we may unmistakably feel a unit consisting of even half a dozen weak elements run very quickly together and followed by an accent member as a genuine iamb" (p. 177). Yet, why the anapest type (u u –) remains a primary pattern in his rhythmic vocabulary in spite of this is never explained.

31. I do not wish to be misunderstood in my argument here. I do not believe that an ideal system ought to reduce all of rhythm to iambs and trochees, as would be implied by a consistent application of the authors' method. Rather, the tendency of the method to have such a result is perhaps the best argument against it, since any analysis based on it becomes overly reductive and not reflective of the realities of rhythmic variety.

accents and weak beats that are created by some aspect of a sound—
its duration, intensity, or pitch—in the context of other sounds.

3. In addition, the theorists of the last three hundred years have
universally understood meter to be a conceptual source of accent
interpretation, a context of regularly recurring structural accents
and weak beats with which, or against which, freer rhythmic designs
may play. The uniquely musical source of meter within individual
compositions, however, remains unclear.

4. Theoretical systems of the recent past have been chiefly interested in three broad aspects of musical motion: the logical form of
rhythmic systems, taxonomies of fundamental rhythmic patterns,
and/or the psychological dynamics of rhythmic phenomena.

To these three interests the present study adds a fourth: an examination of the musical principles by which the parentage of rhythmic
designs may be analytically determined, and a further exploration of
the nature of and relationships between rhythmic levels.[32] The chief
problem in writing such theory arises from the unclear relationship
of pitch interpretation to rhythm interpretation. The criteria of
significance of musical events are clouded by the aforementioned,
circular analytic tendency to value a pitch in terms of its accentual
placement (rhythm-to-pitch) while, at the same time, positing an
accentual scheme on the basis of pitch value (pitch-to-rhythm).
Chapters 3 and 4 of this study, based on the implications of eighteenth century theory, are aimed at establishing a language and a
framework to account for and mediate between these two alterna-
tives.

I would like to stress the formulation "writing theory" as opposed
to "writing a theory" because this study should in no way be con-
strued as the establishment of, much less the attempt to create, a

32. I am not alone in this inquiry. See Peter Westergaard, "Some Problems in Rhythmic
Theory and Analysis," reprinted in *Perspectives on Contemporary Music*, Benjamin Boretz
and Edward T. Cone, eds. (New York, 1972). This contains a short summary and critique of
Cooper's and Meyer's book as well as an investigation of the mechanisms of Webern's
rhythm. See also Allen Forte, "Schenker's Conception of Musical Structure," *JMT*, 3,
no. 1 (1959): 1–30, where Forte suggests that a theory of rhythm for tonal music might
begin by determining the levels at which rhythmic differentiations of Schenkerian pitch
structures become significant. A study that differs markedly from the present one has
been written in response to Forte's suggestion: Anne Alexandra Pierce's "The Analysis
of Rhythm in Tonal Music" (Diss., Brandeis University, 1968).

universal theory of rhythm. It is meant much more as a clarification of the mechanisms of pitch-to-rhythm and rhythm-to-pitch analyses of tonal music and as an attempt to rethink the categories that the traditional literature has devised to describe the rhythmic texture of pieces of music: accent, meter, tempo, and structure. The interdependent relationships of these categories will be examined in order to set the theory of musical rhythm apart from the theory of notation and apart from taxonomies of linguistic verse pattern.[33]

To do this the present study hopes to coexist with past theories that have seen rhythmic configurations as chains of strong- and weak-beat patterns, but it seeks to understand these patterns as they are formed by the interaction of two kinds of levels of motion: (1) the music taken as unaccented, uninterpreted flow, and (2) middle-ground strata that are to be found beneath the level of motion of the musical surface. At these levels, the logical and structural bases by which different rhythmic shapes in a composition relate to one another can be discovered.

33. That notation is not analysis is evident. As for the second model, even given for the moment that architectures of poetic feet may be used to describe individual levels of motion, they cannot mediate between rhythm and pitch without some reference to pitch function. And if such a reference is made, then the musical terminologies of pitch, duration, and accent are sufficient while poetic feet are purely gratuitous, if not misleading, terms based on an analogy that no longer applies.

2

Uninterpreted Rhythmic
Structures

As indicated in the previous chapter, past theories of rhythm have
suggested that the determination of rhythm is largely a matter of
grouping and accent interpretation and that, without such interpretation, there is no rhythm of any aesthetic interest. This would
be especially true in the case of a simple, regular succession of equidurational pulses. Taken as a continuous flow, such pulses suggest
no necessary internal groupings but merely a tempo of recurrence,
and to create rhythmic or metrical motion of any consequence, it
would require the placement of some interpretive accents within the
flow. Should this occur, then any ensuing rhythm may be described
in terms of whatever scheme of accents is used; the pulses become a
significant, interpreted rhythmic structure, where before they were
merely an uninterpreted (i.e., without internal accents) and monot-
onous pattern, unsegmented and presumably of little rhythmic
significance.

In terms of musical compositions, however, the above example is
a rare and simplistic instance. Ordinarily, compositions present
simultaneous strings[1] of varied durational values, varied pitches,
and varied dynamic levels. If these strings are considered before any
judgment is made as regards their internal metrical organization or
any other grouping that may be within them, then they too may be
thought of as being uninterpreted patterns—patterns without strong
and weak beats—but unlike the simple sequence of pulses described
above, these uninterpreted musical strings do have some significant
rhythmic structure.

The pitchless strings of example 2.1 illustrate this principle.

---

1. The word "string" is borrowed from the terminology of computer languages and
denotes merely a succession of literal elements.

Example 2.1

The various interpretations of the first string, listed below it, may all differ in terms of grouping and accent, but they all pertain to an uninterpreted pattern whose logical structure may be minimally described as the regular alternation of the unaccented time values: 1, 2.

The term "rhythmic structures" thus does not simply designate "motives" or *"gestalten,"* although these certainly qualify as structures. Motives and gestalten have been generally characterized as perceived, accentuated patterns of motion from event to event in a string of sounds and rests, each event in the string having a certain moment of beginning, fixed duration and relationship to an accentuation of the whole. Yet interpreted patterns of this kind, like those of example 2.1 (B, C, and D), may also be seen as structured configurations of pure duration and contour—apart from any special scheme of internal accentuation (as in 2.1, A). In this light, they are representative of *uninterpreted rhythmic structures.*

Most work in the theory of rhythm, since Riemann, has been directed towards explicating principles of segmentation, accent, and stress as they relate only to motives and gestalten—to interpreted structures—and this theoretical concentration grows out of the methodology that rhythmic analyses have followed. They begin by viewing the musical composition as its interpreted parts, usually concentrating on motif, melody, and the presence of a notated meter, Meter is understood as a felt, accentual scheme of measurable length apart from the two former categories, which are taken as gestalten— i.e., already interpreted forms. Then a synthesis of interpreted structures is built up, and their shapes are described in general terms—as isomorphic to patterns of poetic feet, for example, or end-, middle-, or beginning-accented forms.

This methodology often runs into difficulty, however, with thick polyphonic textures that do not conform to the scheme of melody plus metric accompaniment. In addition, any viewpoint that considers melody to be a kind of rhythmically stratified polyphony all by itself finds little appropriate explanation of temporal organization in this kind of theory of rhythm.

The intent of the present study is to augment past theories by alternatively approaching the rhythm of a composition in terms of stages of interpretation. With this procedure, the composition is first seen as a long, complex, and uninterpreted summation of all its attacks, durations, and rests. Physically, when any musical work is played, its gross rhythmic structure is in fact the resultant of all its constituent rhythmic patterns.

The next stage is to consider the structure of internally uninterpreted configurations of duration and contour that may be isolated within the whole resultant pattern. Finding such configurations is an act of analysis in which the analyzer discovers by means of certain criteria what is, in effect, a pattern that is contained within a larger pattern, a *rhythmic sub-pattern* of the piece.

Finally the ways in which rhythmic sub-patterns may interact and may be subject to internal accent interpretation must be considered, but it should be pointed out that a comparison of the structures of sub-patterns can be made at any of the stages of the analysis. Hence two highly interpreted patterns that differ may share a common structure when viewed as less-interpreted configurations because the structure of an uninterpreted string of signals does not disappear but is included when that string is accented or combined with others (as in example 2.1).

Here it must be pointed out that this is not a theory of human perception but rather a conceptual model that is designed to implement an analysis of structure. There are, nevertheless, some resemblances to perception. It is true that pieces of music physically present themselves as resultant rhythmic patterns when they are played and that the educated listener performs perceptual analysis and hears inner configurations in music with a skill that seems automatic—once it is acquired. It is not claimed here, however, that the staged methodology described above has a parallel in the mechanisms of human perception but merely that it places itself in a similar position to the music. Because of this, no conclusions will be drawn about the mechanisms of perception. In fact, these mechanisms may well be impediments to seeing hidden correspondences among uninterpreted rhythmic structures because they so often enable us to find, first and immediately, the interpreted structures only.

With no prejudice to additional accent interpretations that may be made later, then, this chapter investigates some of the criteria by which rhythmic sub-patterns may be logically discovered in compositions. To do this, rhythm is considered to be first the rhythm of some thing, not an abstract concept of motion. Further, there can be no rhythm of any single event since there must be at least two events for there to be any measure of motion from one to the other. Thus the logical form of the rhythm of any succession of events hangs on the idea of recurrence and the implications of its definition.

Virtually anything that presents itself to consciousness can be said to have occurred. For an event to recur, there must be some criterion that establishes a logical class of events in which the occurrence and its recurrence are both members. For music, the most inclusive class of typical events contains sounds that are attacked and held for some interval of time and measured moments during which sound is absent The sounds may vary in quality of attack, dynamic level, timbre, pitch class, pitch function, register, density, and duration; these, of course, comprise a list of some further criteria by which recurrent events may be classed.

The following paragraphs more closely consider various criteria of recurrence useful for the discernment of rhythmic sub-patterns in a composition. If events that belong to the same class recur at equal intervals of time, then they define a stratum of motion; they have a simple periodicity for which each new recurrence begins a cycle that ends with the next recurrence. If the intervals of time are unequal, the consequent rhythmic sub-pattern defined by the events is more complex.

1. *Attack point*. Attack point is a criterion that can be used to describe minimally any rhythmic configuration. It simply establishes a class of events such that any attack (any onset or new instance of a sound) belongs to that class, and any attack following some initial attack constitutes a recurrence of the former event.

Taking any string of attacks, an interval of time can be measured between consecutive events by this criterion—an *attack-point interval*. In example 2.2 there is a regularity of time interval between the first eight attacks. The *e* has a different measurable duration until the next four events, which are separated from each other by a new attack-point interval. It can now be seen that this criterion is the one

Strauss/Don Juan

Example 2.2

used to establish the equivalence of the patterns in example 2.1; i.e., they all have the same attack-point rhythm.

The length of time between attack points is not to be confused with the durational value of notes, although the two may easily be equivalent. In example 2.3, they are not always so, and the number under each attack point represents the time value (in eighth notes) until the next attack point.

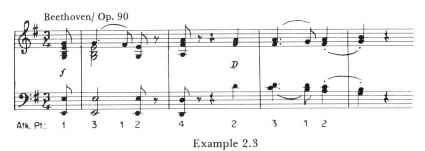

Example 2.3

By itself, attack-point criterion makes no distinction of any rhythmic sub-patterns in the piece. Thus in the following fragment (example 2.4) the rhythm of attack points within the measure is the resultant of 8 against 9 against 10 against 21—a type of configuration that will be dealt with in chapter 5.

Example 2.4

As the attack-point rhythm of example 2.4 characterizes an historically local musical style, the following example represents the
rhythmic style of its age.

Example 2.5

This consistent rate of attacks in regular sixteenth notes is the
reason that Bach's music has so often been used to illustrate the
principle that a sequence of steady pulses must be differentiated by
some other criteria in order to create aesthetically significant rhythm.

For such cases, attack point may indeed be called upon in combination with other criteria. If, for example, two sub-patterns are
determined by a pitch-to-rhythm decision in example 2.5 (i.e., the
lower pitches act in the context of bass-functions; the upper ones do

not) then one can speak of the attack-point rhythm of either the treble or the bass.

To summarize, attack point says nothing of the function, registral location, or duration of pitches and sounds but merely measures the rhythm of their recurrence. Properly speaking, then, this criterion must be used in conjunction with some other, as in the above example, in order to pertain to a rhythmic sub-pattern because alone it will determine the resultant, uninterpreted rhythm of the entire piece. In light of this it can be said that, by itself, the attack-point criterion will always establish the extreme rhythmic foreground of a composition—the absolute surface of articulated movement.

2. *Timbre*. Timbre is the criterion by which rhythmic sub-patterns may be differentiated most easily. By it the qualities of sound made by particular instruments or groups of instruments are classed such that the rhythmic patterns of individual lines are linked to the instruments that play them. These lines are determined, then, by the recurrence of events of the same general timbre.

In the following example the rhythmic patterns of each instrument may be differentiated from the regular, eighth-note motion of the whole attack-point rhythm by timbre alone. For this case, the recurrence of the same timbral events of the first violin establishes a significant stratum of motion that is regular and slower than that of the extreme rhythmic foreground.

Example 2.6

Example 2.7

A change in timbre can also be an event-defining class. It is the logical complement of the timbral recurrence described above in that it pertains to the nonrecurrence of a timbre, and just as a stratum of motion can be determined by sounds made by the same instrument(s), so too can a time interval be measured between each instance of a change in timbre. By the latter criterion there is a stratum of motion in quarter-note values in this extract from the *Rite of Spring* (example 2.7). Here each successive entrance involving a new timbre creates the quarter-note motion.

It should be mentioned that there are cases for which the choice of determining sub-patterns on the basis of timbral similarity or timbral change becomes ambiguous. In the following the differences of timbre within the flute family are likely not rhythmically significant to the passage, and the segment played by each individual instrument is of less rhythmic interest than the summation of the parts. Hence timbral similarity is more important here.[2]

Example 2.8

The case of Webern's Opus 6, no. 1 is problematic, however, and presents a more difficult ambiguity (example 2.9). Here the sub-patterns of timbral similarity are not extensive (there is not yet a rhythmic pattern in the trumpet or horn part); and yet if the passage were segmented according to timbral change, the music would appear to display a rhythmic pointillism (of which it has often been unjustly accused).

2. The same reasoning applies to more recent music in which a muted trumpet may, typically, sound like an oboe. In such cases, the analyst has to evaluate the sound and determine whether the compositional context suggests the situation is one of timbral change or timbral similarity.

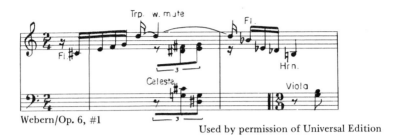

Webern/Op. 6, #1

Example 2.9

Clearly, the attack-point rhythm of this example is of great significance, and any interpretation that would tend conceptually to obscure it on the basis of timbral change is probably a mistake. Nevertheless, it must be recognized that there is a rhythmic sub-pattern
formed on the basis of timbral change, and the analyst may choose
to consider it significant to a later accent and grouping interpretation. For example, groups of attacks of the same timbre might be
seen to coincide with structurally important pitch-class sets in this
example.

   3. *Dynamics.* The rhythmic implications of dynamic change are
often obvious, but there are significant problematic cases. Example
2.10, which is a reduction to attack and stress of example 1.8,
illustrates an uninterpreted rhythmic sub-pattern determined by
the recurrence of dynamic stress. In each case the stress is a change
from the immediately preceding dynamic level, and thus a sub-
pattern is read in terms of the time intervals between recurrent,
non-adjacent attacks of the same loudness.

Stravinsky/ Rite

Example 2.10

   Equivalent change in dynamic level might also be considered a
determinant factor. In the following example, the forte marking is
not nearly so much a sudden stress as it is the upper limit of a crescendo and the beginning of a decrescendo. The passage may be

considered segmented, then, such that the crescendo is an event of dynamic change over time and the decrescendo is a recurrence of such an event. The exact point of division between the two, however, is not theoretically apparent.

Example 2.11

Ignoring for the moment any other aspects of pitch and orchestration that divide the passage more obviously, an idealization of its isolated dynamic form would consider the loudness of its sound to be always changing. Hence, the point of division may exclude the moment of the forte marking and begin with the first signal that alters the direction of dynamic change, or it may include that moment, taken as the beginning of an alteration of direction.

The minimal theoretical requirements for dynamic rhythm are not always clear. The following four figures present dynamic change outside of the context of attack-point rhythm.

A, B, C, D figures

A and B are models of gradual acoustic attack and decay respectively, but though there is a change of dynamic level in each case it is too gradual to divide into separate events. The events for these cases, rather, take the form: silence, sound, silence; and since none of the silences are measured events there is no definitive rhythmic motion. Were the silences of finite measure, however, a time interval could be found to describe the rhythm of their recurrence (e.g.,).

Because figure C indicates a sudden dynamic change, it is a case for which two segments may be postulated: (1) the time interval between the attack and the inception of the new dynamic level, and (2) the time interval between the first instance of the new dynamic level and the silence following the end of the signal. This and figure D (which has a similar analysis to that of example 2.11) are perhaps the lower limits of determining sub-patterns based on dynamic criteria.[3]

The rhythmic significance of a single stress, not in the context of any other stresses, should be considered in light of the above discussion. Technically a single stress will be followed by a recurrence of the dynamic level that immediately precedes it, but if such a segmentation is not linked to other significant criteria, the stress will function more coloristically and rhetorically than it will to establish any extensive sub-pattern. The more common instance of a stress is in combination with others, as illustrated in the following examples.

In example 2.12 two dynamic sub-patterns create two strata of motion that are characteristic of the mazurka. The first is a sub-pattern of stressed upbeats separated by a time interval equal to six quarter notes. The second is a sub-pattern of stressed upbeats separated by the equivalent of three quarter notes. What characterizes the mazurka as a rhythmic form is the displacement of these two chains of dynamic events with respect to the chain of recurrent entrances of the bass notes at the beginning of each measure.

Chopin/Mazurka, Op. 6, #1

Example 2.12

3. The opposite of C $\displaystyle{d \atop \boldsymbol{p}\ subito\,\boldsymbol{f}}$ is not considered here because the dynamic change amounts to a new attack and therefore implies an attack-point rhythm.

In example 2.13 a stratum of uninterpreted motion (3 3 3) is initiated by a regular alternation of forte and piano dynamic levels. That this motion is uninterpreted must be emphasized. Questions about the presence of $\frac{2}{4}$ meter and its effect on accentual grouping in this composition pertain to the interpretation of sub-patterns—to accentual schemes within them. For the moment, the structure of this fragment has not been exhaustively described but only has been found to contain a sub-pattern on the basis of multiple dynamic stresses.[4]

Used by permission of Universal Edition

Example 2.13

4. *Density*. This criterion may give rise to a sub-pattern with reference to either the density of simultaneous attacks or the density of simultaneous sub-patterns. The following fragment from Bach's Cantata no. 65 is an example of the former type: a rhythmic sub-pattern brought out by changes in the density of simultaneous attacks (example 2.14).[5]

4. The linkage of certain interval classes to a scheme of duple time is discovered in this composition and discussed in David Lewin, "A Metrical Problem in Webern's Op. 27," *JMT* 6, no. 1 (1962): 125 ff.

5. In this style, such changes in density are equivalent to changes of orchestral timbre and changes of dynamic level. Another example of the rhythmic implications of density recurrence and changes in the density of simultaneous attacks can be observed in mm. 26–61 of Krzysztof Penderecki's *To the Victims of Hiroshima: Threnody for 52 Stringed Instruments*.

Bach/ Cantata No. 65, Aria

Example 2.14

The manner in which density relates not to simultaneous attacks
but instead to the combination of sub-patterns in a piece is more
complex. As the extreme rhythmic foreground, attack-point rhythm
is the uninterpreted summation of all possible sub-patterns in a composition. Any addition of a sub-pattern to an already established
texture, or deletion therefrom, for that matter, effects a change in
the density of sub-patterns that makes up the texture.

The entrances of new parallel voices (orchestral unison or octave
doubling) or of new contrapuntal voices (determined by pitch-to-
rhythm criteria) create a rhythm of change in the density of sub-
patterns. The fourth measure in example 2.15 illustrates the
difference between the density of simultaneous attacks and the
density of sub-patterns. Here there are three sub-patterns in spite of
the fact that not every attack point is characterized by three simultaneous attacks.

48

Bach/ WTC, Vol. I, xix

Example 2.15

Renaissance music furnishes many obvious examples of rhythmic strata that are brought out by the additions of sub-patterns to a texture. In the following, the entrances of vocal sub-patterns create a stratum of motion that coincides with the rate of succession of whole notes. In effect, each new voice entrance is separated from the immediately preceding voice entrance by a distance of a whole note.

Example 2.16

Density pertains, then, either to the combination of attacks or to the combination of apparently independent strings that are isolated by timbre, counterpoint, or register.

5. *Pattern recurrence.* Pattern recurrence takes any sub-pattern and makes it a class to which any further instance of the sub-pattern belongs. Strings of pattern recurrences in regular cycles, like the one in example 2.17, establish a rhythm of recurrence that is slower than the attack-point rhythm of the foreground. Here a rhythmic pattern recurs at intervals equal to six quarter notes.

Example 2.17

It would be impossible to list all conceivable kinds of patterns, but a discussion of the general criteria useful for their discovery is warranted.

First, patterns can be made up of identically ordered strings of durational values. Example 2.17 serves as an illustration of this.

Second, pattern can arise from some regular ordering of time intervals between attack points. As indicated by the brackets in example 2.18, recurrent patterns may be created by various interpretations. Intervals of time between recurrent patterns are designated here in quantities of eighth notes.

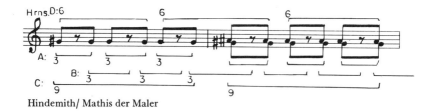

Hindemith/ Mathis der Maler

Example 2.18

In example 2.18, the first two attack points may be taken as a pattern that repeats (A), or the second and third may qualify as a repeating pattern (B). In addition, groups of smaller sub-patterns may themselves sum to larger patterns that repeat (C and D). To paraphrase Hauptmann, then, the determination of recurrent patterns depends upon where one considers them to begin. The specification of one pattern to the exclusion of another by interpretive accent is considered in the next chapter. For now, examples such as 2.18 are considered as uninterpreted entities whose structure is a ground for the accentuated sub-patterns that may later be shown to be within them.

Third, pattern is often a function of some pitch-contour that may coincide with an ordered string of durations or attack points. The above examples already demonstrate this to some extent. The opening of the second movement of Mahler's First Symphony here further illustrates the variety of latent strata of motion that can arise by pattern and contour recurrence and be literally represented in a composition.

Mahler/Symphony #1: II

Example 2.19

In the bass part alone, for instance, some of these strata are determined by the following:

1. The first two bars contain a pattern of varied durational values linked to the pitch contour. This is repeated by the next two bars.

2. The attack-point rhythm of the first bar, linked to pitch con-

tour, is a sub-pattern of the second bar. By this criterion, the second bar is a recurrence of the first; i.e., its foreground rhythm is different but the attack and contour pattern of the first bar is included within it.

3. The odd-numbered bars create a stratum of motion by the recurrence of the durational pattern of the first bar.

4. The even-numbered bars create a chain of patterns whose beginning is displaced with respect to the chain formed by the odd-numbered bars. (Similarly, the violins can be read from ♩♩♪ to ♩♩♪, or from β to β, or in terms of the combined pattern: ♩♩♪ β.)

Relationships like these are often obvious and may appear trivial, but they perform a vital function in saturating compositions with represented rhythmic strata. In fact, Riepel's correction of his student's composition (example 2.20) addresses itself to precisely the creation of these kinds of interrelated levels of motion as determined by pattern.

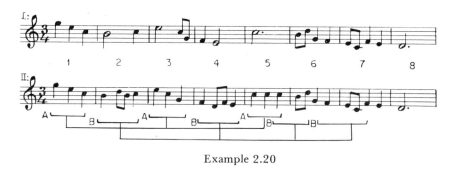

Example 2.20

Here his corrected version (II) establishes a pattern recurrence in each of the first three odd-numbered measures (A), a chain of recurrent patterns in the first two even-numbered measures (B), and a durational pattern (bars 1 and 2) that repeats after two measures (bars 3 and 4). The alteration of measure 5 is a good example of the continuance of a scheme of pattern recurrence. By changing the rhythmic content of the bar, Riepel is filling up the rhythmic strata of the composition with structures that represent them. Furthermore, the determination of pattern here is not simply metrical and defined by the bar lines since the sub-patterns marked "B" in the example are identical to each other when taken as uninterpreted strings.

These two examples indicate how rhythmic structures are aesthetically organized in compositions. The opening bar in the second movement of Mahler's First Symphony, for instance, shows how any sub-pattern represented in the piece can momentarily become the foreground rhythm. As for the reduplication of pattern within each of these two examples, it not only establishes a level of motion but it is, in itself, the source of a homogeneity of rhythmic design and thus of compositional coherence.

This last point merits special emphasis and expansion. For the purposes of analysis, the recurrence of a pattern can be considered valid for a temporal augmentation or diminution of a particular pattern—whether it is linked or unlinked with pitch contour. In the following often-cited example, the coherence of design in disparate movements of a symphony is based on the proportional identity of two attack-point patterns, although the tempos of performance for A and B are different (example 2.21). This kind of pattern recurrence

Atk. Pt: 1 1 1   1 1 1
Beethoven/ 5th Symphony

Example 2.21

is not necessarily rhythm-producing, but it is vital to comparative analysis, since it establishes formal relationships of identity between designs that operate on different rhythmic strata of a piece.

It should be pointed out here that the identity of the two patterns in example 2.21 is based on the three time intervals between the first four signals in each case, and not on the durations of the final, held notes, which differ in the two movements. The intent here is not to warp time values and speak of a general, accentual similarity but rather to compare patterns that are identical except for tempo. To do otherwise would be to sacrifice the uniqueness of the two rhythmic designs on the altar of analytic convenience and to blur the distinction between general similarity and proportional identity.

The subject of the present chapter has been the derivation of rhythmic events and the discovery of the strata of their recurrence by five criteria headings: attack point, timbre, dynamics, density, and pattern recurrence.[6] In the analysis of relatively pitchless music, played by drum orchestras and the like, these criteria are the ones that are principally used to determine slower-moving rhythmic configurations that combine to produce a rhythmic foreground. In music that is dependent upon pitch systems, however, and especially in the context of tonal music, other criteria, indicative of the recurrence of pitches having the same level of significance, can be used in conjunction with the above five. The following chapter considers this further area of inquiry.

6. Other criteria that do not necessarily involve specific pitches, such as registral recurrence, demand similar analytic procedures; i.e., the criterion defines a class, and a rhythm of recurrent events belonging to that class may then be specified.

3

The Nature of
Stratification with
Respect to Pitch

PITCH LEVELS

The notion that pitch configurations may generate rhythmic structures has been shown to be at least as old as the eighteenth-century
analyses of compound lines made by Heinichen. In its most general
form, this principle rests on the recognition that a rhythmic sub-
pattern may be derived from a gross, attack-point rhythm by either
of two criteria: (1) the recurrence of a pitch, or (2) the occurrence of
a pitch event that corresponds to a prior pitch event of the same level
of significance.

In terms of simple pitch recurrence, no consideration of pitch
function is required. Thus, in the following example a regular motion
may be ascertained by the recurrence of the *b-flats* in the treble at a
time interval of three quarter notes (example 3.1).

Example 3.1

Here, as is often the case, this rate of pitch recurrence is supple-
mented by the rate of recurrence of the left hand accompanimental
scheme within each measure.

Rhythmic strata that arise from the simple recurrences of pitches,
however, are more often than not ambiguous and even misleading

when they are found in tonal music if they are not based on an evaluation of a pitch's function within the context of a composition. If,
for example, the repetition of the *a*'s were considered significant to
the motion of Riepel's "Vierer," the resulting rhythmic sub-pattern
would represent a fairly exotic reading of the passage (example 3.2).

Example 3.2

As stated previously, this example can be better understood if the
pitches are assigned to levels of significance; one level includes relatively stable pitches while excluding those tones that embellish or
pass between the stable pitches—yet another level might include precisely the addition of the embellishing tones.

The outer voices of example 3.2 might then be seen to contain, on
this basis, a stable *c* and a stable *b-flat*, both of which serve an important function within the dominant harmony until the resolution
to the *a* in bar 4 (a motion which negates the stability of the *b-flat*)
and to the *f* in that same bar (which supplants the initial *c* as the bass
tone of primary importance). A rhythmic sub-pattern by such parentage is displayed in example 3.3, A.

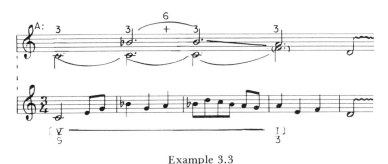

Example 3.3

Here, the sub-pattern referred to is expressed numerically in quantities of quarter notes (3 3 3 3).[1]

---

1. Again, this is not the only possible harmonization of the passage, but Riepel's examples are being considered here as complete and written for an unaccompanied solo instrument. Alternate harmonizations might very well lead to different analyses.

The reading of the fourth measure requires explanation. Why has the *f* been shifted onto the first beat of the measure instead of being allowed to remain in its place on the third beat? Is not the third beat, after all, the arrival of the bass tone and thus as rhythmically significant as the arrival on the *a* in the same measure? An answer to these questions is provided by asking another: Is the *a* in bar 4 to be heard as being supported by a tonic *f* on the first beat, or must it wait until the third beat to gain that meaning? Clearly if the *a* is stable on the first beat this stability implies support by a tonic *f*; and if it is read as being unstable, then such assumption of a tonic *f* on the first beat is not warranted.

There is a paradoxical aspect to the fourth measure that beclouds a reading of its rhythmic significance. A rhythmic sub-pattern is being derived in this example on the basis of the recurrence of pitch events having roughly the same stability. Although the dominant function is clearly less stable than the tonic, stability here refers to pitches that are stable within either of those harmonies while it is operative. On the one hand, the *a* in bar 4 is considered stable, and so the implied presence of a tonic *f* beneath it is required. On the other hand, the *a* cannot be considered to be stable until the *f* is heard on the third beat. A simple permutation of the pitch content of this bar, followed by an *f,*

changes the reading of the *a* completely and illustrates why, in this case, the *f* must be heard on the third beat if the *a* is to be stable (the *e* must be enclosed by the *a* and the *f*).

One is forced to the conclusion here that a proper analysis of rhythmic sub-patterns depends upon the total context of a pitch's placement; the presence of a tonic *f*, in example 3.3, on the first beat of m. 4 is implied precisely because that *f* is supplied in another place (on the third beat) and is itself followed by a pitch event that indicates a new area of stability. Hence the effect of the contextual placement of the *f* on the third beat of the measure is reflexive and directs the meaning of that pitch back to the first beat of the measure. For the discovery of rhythmic sub-patterns on the basis of pitch function, then, the assumed presence of a pitch in one place, on the basis of its later appearance at another place, will be considered as being *reflexively determined.*

Two additional sub-patterns remain to be discussed in example 3.3. The one already determined above is based on events of equivalent stability within their respective harmonic areas. A second rhythmic sub-pattern may be read on the basis of the first appearance of any relatively stable pitch events. By this criterion, the repetition of the *b-flat* in the third measure really supplies nothing new to the tonal structure, and thus it may be considered as tied to the second bar— producing the sub-pattern 3 6 3.

On a deeper level of structural meaning even this first *b-flat* may be considered subordinate to the primary harmonic motion in the bass—V–I—which creates a sub-pattern of 9–3, or a long dotted rhythm (𝅗𝅥. 𝅘𝅥). Here again the tonic function of the fourth measure is reflexively determined to extend through the whole measure (shown below the example).

All of the three rhythmic strata in example 3.3 are determined by levels of pitch significance, and they are accompanied by another sub-pattern created by a pattern recurrence linked to contour—the second and fourth measures. These sub-patterns illustrate the principle that a rhythmic stratum may be regular and periodic (3 3 3 3) or may be irregular (3 6 3; 9 3). Furthermore, none of the pitch strata alone constitutes the foreground motion of the passage, and as such, these strata illustrate a further principle: any pitch reduction of a composition will have an overall motion from event to event that is slower than the rate of recurrence of attack points on the rhythmic foreground.

The theorist most responsible for the discovery and elucidation of structural levels like these in tonal music was Heinrich Schenker. In his numerous writings[2] Schenker provided not only a theoretical

---

2. I include here a partial list of Schenker's main writings, based on David Beach's article "A Schenker Bibliography," *JMT* 13, no. 1 (1967): 2 ff., which provides a complete list.

1906 *Neue musikalische Theorien und Phantasien, Vol. I: Harmonielehre.* Vienna: Universal Edition.

1910 *Neue musikalische Theorien und Phantasien, Vol. II, Part I: Kontrapunkt (Cantus Firmus und zweistimmiger Satz).* Vienna: Universal Edition.

1922 *Neue musikalische Theorien und Phantasien, Vol. II, Part 2: Kontrapunkt (Drei und mehrstimmiger Satz).* Vienna: Universal Edition.

1925–1930 *Das Meisterwerk in der Musik.* Munchen: Drei Masken Verlag.

basis for understanding tonal music in terms of levels but also an analytic and graphic technique, as well as a specialized vocabulary, for the description of such levels within works of music.

At the heart of Schenker's thought is the idea that pieces of tonal music do not merely juxtapose repetitions and variations of disparate motives but that they proceed organically to unfold linearly or to arpeggiate, at various levels, the principal triad that is itself the tonality of any individual composition. Hence motives and themes may themselves be seen against a background of pitch configurations that are more structurally vital to the composition; and indeed these motives and themes may be shown to be comprehensible in terms of Schenker's levels.

This study relies on Schenkerian techniques, in that it is concerned with rhythmic strata created by pitch levels, and so a further illustration of the discovery of such rhythmic strata will be provided here by Schenker's own prefatory analysis of Bach's C-minor fugue (example 3.4):

Example 3.4

With only a few exceptions, which contain their own justification, Bach's fugue subjects display a strictly enclosed situation. A suitable example of this is the subject of the C-minor fugue which is to be understood by the following illustration:

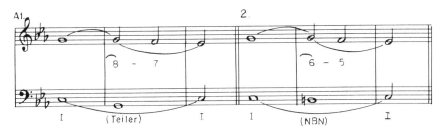

Jahrbuch I, 1925.
Jahrbuch II, 1926.
Jahrbuch III, 1930.

1935 *Neue musikalische Theorien und Phantasien, Vol. III: Der Freie Satz.* Two volumes: I, Text; II, Musical Figures. Vienna: Universal Edition.
Second edition, edited and revised by Oswald Jonas, 1956.

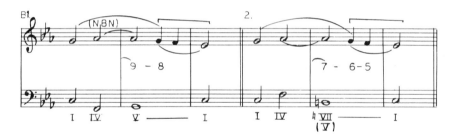

The determining content of the subject is a descent through a third:
g-f-e-flat (Example A). The lower voice of this fundamental structure
supplies either the root of a dividing dominant (A,1) or the third built
on that root (A,2). The latter case, because it is melodically a second,
has more the effect of a neighbor [adjacent] note than that of a true
dividing dominant.

In Example B, for a heightening of expression, the originally stationary *g*
is unfolded by means of a neighbor note [*a-flat*] that is itself accompanied
by its own bass tone (a IV harmony). As the case may apply to either the
root (B,1) or the third of V (B,2), this consequently leads to either a 9–8
or a 7–6 suspension that further intensifies the heightening of expression
already provided by the neighbor note.

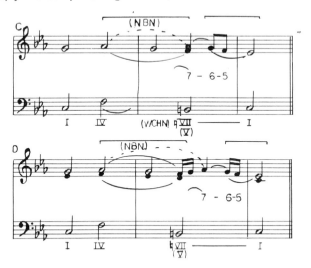

In Example C, we observe how the neighboring *a-flat* is itself expressed by
a descent through a third: *a-flat-g-f*. In continuation of the first half-note *g*
this descent moves in half-notes—placing the middle passing tone [*g*] on the
downbeat of m. 2 and thereby making it an accented passing note [Wechsel-

note]. Under these circumstances, however, the reading of Example B and of the fundamental structure [A] can only be regained by an overlapping *a-flat* on the third beat of m. 2 that is linked to the former *a-flat* (see the dotted slur in the sketch). Only now, because of the broadening effect of the first descent of a third [*a-flat-g-f*] the second [*g-f-e-flat*] must become contracted and must move in eighth-notes. Between these two descents of a third there is a parallelism that is especially intensified by the intrusion of the second descent [*g-f-e-flat*]. This principal descent (compare it with Example A) remains operative then—in spite of its shortened time values in Example C and in spite of the fact that it first appears to present itself as a mere imitation of the immediately preceding descent of a third from *a-flat*. It takes priority as the determinant meaning of the passage because of the parallelism, the suspension, and the motion from V to I.

In Example D, an inner voice—*f-e-flat-d*—is seen to form parallel thirds with the main descent from *g*. On the downbeat of m. 2, the *e-flat* shares the accented passing note character of the *g*. Moreover, the overlapping *a-flat* in m. 2 is now replaced by the slide-like, upward-turning phrase: *f-g-a-flat*. . . . In light of this, it is necessary to give the *a-flat* a quarter-note value in order to obtain the effect of linking the two instances of *a-flat* and thus the effect of a 7–6 suspension (in the same sense as the voice leading of level C). The effect of this linkage is gained by the greater duration of the quarter-note value.[3]

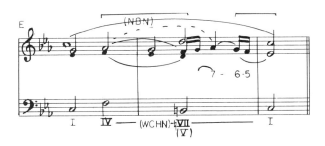

3. Here I take issue with Schenker's observation. The linkage of the two *a-flats* may be obscured by allowing the second one a lesser time value, e.g.:

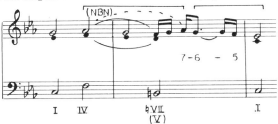

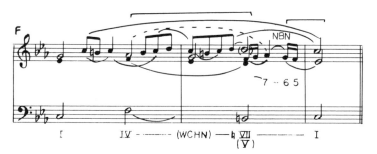

Next, in Example E, there is a superimposition of a fourth voice which alternates a motion to with a return from a neighbor note in long note values: *c-d-c*.

In Example F, this neighbor note is unfolded in smaller neighbor note figures which avail themselves now of the lower, now of the upper neighbor. (See the small slurs drawn either below or above these motions in the sketch.) This highest voice is really a neighbor note motion signifying only a stationary tone, and against the motion of the middle voice, it seems to fade in importance.

This then is the origin and content of the fugue subject at one and the same time. All of the structural levels, displayed from A to F in the illustration, are contained within the final monophonic form of the fugue subject. In it the two highest voices are easily to be recognized while, in contrast, the configuration of the lower voices proceeds—in concealed fashion—as the only possible one.[4]

A commentary on this analysis will clarify some theoretical considerations that are germane to this chapter. First it is important to understand that Schenker does not value one of the structural levels to the exclusion of the others. They are all constituents of the "final monophonic form" of the fugue subject.

Second, the sketches may be read from background (A) through various middleground levels up to the foreground. Such a generative reading shows how each level adds only those notes that are directly attached to notes of the immediately preceding level. To jump from level A to level D, for example, would be incorrect because there is

---

but it is not obliterated. Granted that this counterexample is inelegant, it would nonetheless appear that the *a-flats* are still linked, the 7–6 suspension still operates, and the notion that a pitch's tonal function depends on its duration is a questionable one—even when it is implied by Schenker.

4. This analysis is translated from *Das Meisterwerk in der Musik*, Jahrbuch II, pp. 60–62.

not yet an *a-flat* on the former level, and thus the first span of a third on the latter level would have an unclear point of attachment to the music. Hence the essence of musical structure is apparently contained not only on individual levels but also in the relationships between the levels.

Third, the sketches may be read from foreground to background. This is a degenerative (or reductive) reading, and as Allen Forte has concisely written:

> Reduction is approximately the reverse of variation. By means of variation technique, a basic structure becomes more elaborate, in terms of increasing number of melodic-rhythmic elements. Reduction accomplishes the reverse; detail is gradually eliminated in accord with the traditional distinction between dissonant and consonant tones (made with reference to the tonic triad, the element of consonance) so that the underlying, controlling structure is revealed.[5]

Fourth, the concept of prolongation operates on the basis of the above distinction between levels. Thus the *g* on level A is prolonged by the upper neighbor *a-flat* of level B—which momentarily replaces the *g* on a more foreground level; and this *a-flat* is itself prolonged by the span: *a-flat-g-f* on level C. On one level, then, a pitch (*g*) is being prolonged while on another level it is a passing tone and functions to prolong its own neighbor.

Finally, the six levels that Schenker describes pertain only to the subject of the fugue. In the context of the entire composition even level A is a middleground and prolongs an essentially stable *c*, the first scale step of the tonic key. The ensuing fugal answer prolongs the fifth scale step of the tonic key, *g*, and Schenker indicates this by his final analytic sketch, shown here in example 3.5.

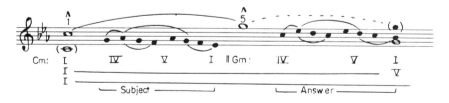

Example 3.5

Here the fugue subject and answer are shown, effectively, to com-

5. Forte, *JMT* 3, no. 1 (1959): 14–15.

prise an ascent from the first to the fifth scale step ($\hat{1}$ and $\hat{5}$ in the sketch). Note how the slurs in this sketch indicate the two descents of a third (from *a-flat* and from *g*) and how three levels of harmonic motion are indicated beneath the staff.

Schenker has often been accused of ignoring rhythm because of two aspects of his thinking. The first is his concept of the *Ursatz*, an overarching fundamental structure that describes the extreme origin of pieces of tonal music as a linear descent from $\hat{3}$ (or $\hat{5}$ or $\hat{8}$) to $\hat{1}$ over a bass arpeggiation of the tonic triad. The concept of this structure is indeed arhythmic but only because it is posited by Schenker as a schema whose general form is made manifest in specific rhythmic values by the backgrounds of individual pieces. In this sense, the Ursatz is no less a schema than the typical harmonic form of a blues or the common I–VI–IV–V of rock music of the late 1950s. If anything, it is less tied to specific rhythmic expression than these two examples; perhaps a better analogy for the Ursatz would be that of a physiological scheme. The heartbeat, for example, is structured by a certain necessary succession of events even though the precise temporal value of each event may differ from one case to another.

The second aspect of Schenker's thinking that appears to imply an arhythmic reading of music is illustrated by the sketch in example 3.5. For the purpose of graphically assigning a relative weight to pitches, Schenker gives the prolonged tones a greater durational value and the prolonging tones a lesser durational value.

In terms of rhythmic strata, this is correct and necessary because each deeper level is a further reduction of a prior one; it will display fewer events that are generally separated from each other by more time, and this can be efficiently indicated by longer note values. In sketches such as example 3.5, however, the maximum durational value used is a whole note which indicates a symbolically great length of time rather than the span of a single measure of music.

This graphic technique does not thereby mitigate the importance, or awareness, of real time durational values within pitch levels. In fact, Schenker's pitch levels, from A to F, are themselves rhythmic sub-patterns that constitute rhythmic strata; and Schenker indicates as much in his discussion of this point in *Der freie Satz*:

> In the middleground every individual sub-level has a unique rhythm which is in accord with its contrapuntal content. Thus, rhythm progresses through

various prolongational stages until it reaches the foreground, just as do meter and form, which also represent consequences of a progressive contrapuntal differentiation.[6]

To summarize, then, thematic shapes in tonal music are not merely unique successions from note to note but are, in addition, the products of tonal events that occur at different levels. Consequently, the designs of rhythmic foregrounds are not merely successions of syllable-like units but are also the products of deeper rhythmic strata. The sub-patterns on these deeper strata may correspond to the recurrences of dynamic, timbral, or other kinds of events described in chapter two, and they may also correspond to the recurrence of pitch events of equivalent significance at any particular pitch level—as illustrated by the six incremental rhythmic sub-patterns formed by Schenker's levels A through F above.

The meaning of rhythmic strata as they relate to pitch levels has further implications. The sub-patterns discussed in chapter two were described as being uninterpreted, with no comment as regards their metric positions or internal, accentual groupings. In light of Schenker's levels, however, an examination of meter and accent interpretation is now required.

The Interaction of Strata

It will be helpful here to explore first the commonly held notion that periodic and regular motion is metric, while irregular configurations of different time values are rhythmic. This definition is held by Cooper, Meyer, Hauptmann, and Riemann but does not provide sufficient grounds for distinguishing meter from rhythm.

The reason for this insufficiency is that any regularly recurring pulse, whether considered conceptually or whether represented by musical events, will indicate no other motion except an infinite recurrence when it is considered by itself (example 3.6).

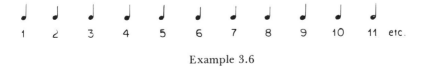

Example 3.6

---

6. Translated by A. Forte from *Der freie Satz*, p. 68. Schenker's discussion of rhythm is contained in sections 284–300 of *Der freie Satz*.

In order to create some regular grouping of elements within a simple pulse, there must be some event occurring at regular intervals within it. Such an event may be sounded in the music, or it may be a purely conceptual division of the pulse[7] (example 3.7).

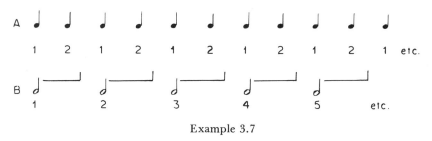

Example 3.7

Here the conceptual act of considering the pulses of level A in pairs occurs once for every two pulses of level A. This recurrent act of grouping, whether it is conceptual or whether it is represented by something in the music, then becomes a pulse itself (B), having a rate of recurrence that is necessarily slower than the rate of level A.

The fundamental logical requirement for meter is therefore that there be a constant rate within a constant rate—at least two rates of events of which one is faster and another is slower.

In view of these two necessary rhythmic strata, the question must now be asked: On which level does the meter appear—on level A or on level B? Clearly there is no meter on level A since, by itself, it is ungrouped. Furthermore there is no meter on level B since, by itself, it is a simple pulse with no slower rate of events (conceptual or otherwise) by which it may be grouped. There is apparently, then, no such thing as a level of meter or a level on which meter may appear; but rather, meter is an outgrowth of the interaction of two levels—two differently-rated strata, the faster of which provides the elements and the slower of which groups them.

This principle, that meter logically requires two levels of motion, neither of which alone can produce it, has significance for the accentual interpretation of pitch levels. As indicated formerly, the fastest articulated musical motion will occur at the absolute surface

7. The reason such an event may be conceptual rather than sounded has to do with typical cases in which a meter is assumed to operate even though some aspect of the music momentarily plays against it. In such cases, a meter is conceptually supplied.

of a composition. Since this rhythmic foreground cannot move slower than itself it can manifest no internal rhythmic groupings by itself, and so no meter can exist at this level. The extreme foreground is accentually uninterpreted by definition.

It has also been indicated previously, however, that each increasingly reductive pitch level will contain fewer events spaced further apart, in general; and so it can be expected that meter may arise by the interaction of the foreground with a slower middleground level, or between two middleground levels, or between middleground and background.

Yet behind any background there is only the ultimate structure of a tonal composition, the tonic triad itself. This is a single event that is considered to be prolonged throughout the entire composition. Because it has no rhythm of recurrence, the one theoretical instance of this chord cannot group the elements of the background, and so the concept of meter on the background is meaningless since there is no slower rate by which successive events of the background may be metrically grouped.

The following figure summarizes the above: a meter will never appear on any single stratum, but it will arise from the interaction of two strata, one of which must always be a middleground level.[8]

Figure 1.1

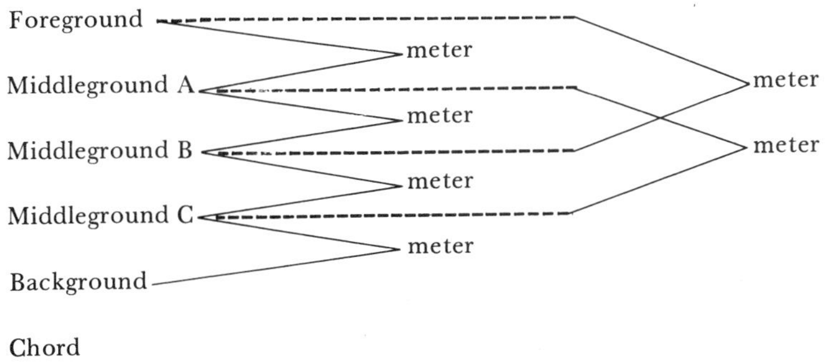

The rhythmic function of middleground strata now becomes more

8. The single exception to this is the interaction of the foreground with the background. On the large scale of most compositions, it would seem that a meter arising from the interaction of these two levels would not be highly significant, since background events are so widely spaced.

obvious. When considered abstractly, a faster level of motion is observed to be grouped (or meter-defined) by a slower motion from event to event on another stratum. Similarly, the uninterpreted foregrounds of tonal compositions may be observed to be grouped by regularly recurring events of slower-moving middlegrounds. Hence the middleground is the interpretation of the foreground; it provides the accents by which foreground events may be grouped.

This function is illustrated in example 3.8.

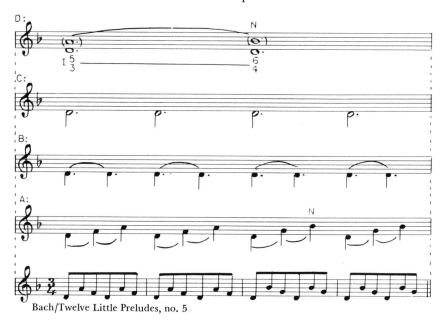

Bach/Twelve Little Preludes, no. 5

Example 3.8

The saturation of rhythmic strata by various middleground structures in this example makes it particularly relevant to a discussion of meter.

First, the extreme rhythmic foreground here is a consistent pulse of eighth notes.

Level A is a middleground arpeggiation of the tonic triad, followed by the same structure with an upper neighbor replacement for the fifth scale step. The creation of this motion is purely pitch-to-rhythm in that the succession of quarter note values corresponds precisely to the elements of arpeggiation. If this arpeggiation is not conceived,

there is no guarantee (or reason) that any quarter note motion
will be comprehended. Further, the rate of each new recurrence
of the arpeggiation is shown on level C. The meter signature of the
piece is therefore strongly represented by the interaction of level
A with level C. Level A interprets the foreground as recurring groups
of two eighth notes each; and level C interprets level A as recurring
groups of three quarter notes each. Hence the two middleground
strata shape the metrical accentuation of the foreground.

The dotted quarter note hemiola motion of level B corresponds
to the rate of recurrence of the triadic pattern of the first three
eighth notes of the piece. The conflict that this middleground stratum creates with level A arises from its obvious pitch inaction. Where
level A interprets the foreground as an arpeggiation, level B interprets the foreground as a static *d*. The structural relationship of
level A to level B is best left to the following chapter. For the moment it is sufficient to be aware of and to make mention of both
these levels.

Level C has already been shown to be the rate of repetition of the
arpeggios of level A. It is also the rate of pattern recurrence, linked
to contour, of the pattern formed by the content of the whole first
measure.

Level D is representative of the overarching motion from the fifth
scale step to the upper neighbor *b-flat* (5–6). As in example 3.3,
these two pitch events are reflexively determined to begin on the
first beats of m. 1 and m. 3 respectively.[9]

9. An analysis of this example appears on p. 42 of Cooper and Meyer, *The Rhythmic
Structure of Music*.

Note how, in m. 1, Cooper and Meyer identify the *f* as the unaccented member of a trochee
on their level 'i', and the *a* as the unaccented member of a trochee on their level '1', when it
is precisely these pitches that must be (to use their definition of accent) "marked for consciousness" if there is to be a level of motion that corresponds to the demands of the notated meter. The presumption of a trochaic pattern on their level '2' suggests that this
metric archetype permeates all the levels of the piece, but this is wholly insupportable
and arbitrary. It could be just as easily claimed that m. 1 is an upbeat to m. 2 (u - rather

At this point the most important question to be asked involves the alternate grouping of level B. Why is this not a valid accentual interpretation, and what is the precise relationship of the notated meter to conflicting middleground interpretations? The case is not always as clear as it is in this example. If the compositional intent is an essentially static d, with triadic embellishments, then a $\frac{6}{8}$ meter is called for (example 3.9) and the reading of level B is relevant. But if the essential musical motion is intended as a purposeful sweep from root to third to fifth of the tonic triad, then the $\frac{3}{4}$ time signature is more appropriate.

Example 3.9

One should not conclude from this, however, that the middleground is created by the meter. Quite to the contrary, the composer has presumably conceived not only of an uninterpreted foreground articulation of the music but also of a middleground that shapes it. The time signature represents nothing more than a graphic technology that helps to indicate which particular middleground structure is meant to shape the foreground. In short, the structure and conception of music clearly precede its notation,[10] and the choice of

---

than -u). Cooper's and Meyer's concept of levels here violates the fundamental logic of accentuation. As revealed by the discussion of meter in the present study, no single level can group itself or can contain both accented and unaccented elements. The presence of multiple accents is a consequence of the interaction of at least two levels, neither of which is accented by itself. In all cases the faster level provides recurrent elements, while events on the slower level mark off points of recurrent groupings of those elements. Cooper and Meyer appear to attest to this in their definition of meter: "Meter is the measurement of the number of pulses between more or less regularly recurring accents" (p. 4). Yet they fail to see that the meter is neither the pulses nor the level of recurrence of the accents but is, rather, the interaction of the two.

10. A composed musical structure determines its own general notation unless the notation is given a will and personality of its own. Aleatoric music may be determined by decisions made by a score that is allowed to conspire with the laws of chance. Perhaps a better statement of the principle is: the degree to which a composer determines the total structure of the music is the degree to which music determines the notational form it takes.

time signature is contingent upon the composition of deeper pitch strata of purposeful motion—and not *vice versa*.

The reason the situation may appear to be the reverse is that the act of reading music often creates the impression that a meter is superimposed on a rhythmic configuration. But this is an impossibility. The only thing resembling meter that can be superimposed on a rhythmic configuration is a stratum of regular motion; and meter has been shown to be an analytic conclusion—not a cause—of the interaction of such a stratum of regular motion with a rhythmic configuration.

In his dissertation on harmonic rhythm,[11] Carl Haenselman discusses a musical passage that will be used here to illustrate the central problem of level B in example 3.8. Simply put, if a foreground rhythm may be grouped by either of two different slower rates of motion (level A or B), why is one preferable and to be understood as the principal metric indicator? Haenselman interprets the rhythm of example 3.10 as a change of harmony at each chord. Significantly, this rhythm of harmonic change is indistinguishable from the attack-point rhythm of the example.

Example 3.10

A rhythmic stratification of the passage, however, examines the significant middleground motion within individual voices and yields the following:

11. Carl Ferdinand Haenselman, "Harmonic Rhythm in Selected Works of the Latter Half of the Nineteenth Century" (Diss., Indiana University, 1966). The example is quoted by Haenselman from Norman Cazden's "The Principle of Direction in the Motion of Similar Tonal Harmonies," *JMT* 2, no. 2 (1958): 162 ff.

Example 3.11

The foreground establishes an attack-point rhythm of regular quarter-note motion.

Level A indicates the essential motion of the phrase—a descent of a third from *g*, during which the *g* is momentarily replaced by its upper neighbor, *a*. The resemblance to Schenker's analysis of the C-minor fugue subject is apparent.

Level B is the rhythm of an inner voice that forms parallel thirds with the essential descent of level A. The motion of level B clearly brings out the implicit regularity of level A and hence an interpretation of the foreground in terms of duple values.

Level C is a superimposed level of motion that moves to an upper neighbor and returns. To paraphrase Schenker, it is essentially a stationary tone: *c*. Note the descent of a third that prolongs the upper neighbor, *d*, for three beats (making the enclosed *c* an accented passing tone). This level provides a potential metric grouping, since the functional tones—*c* and *d*—move in dotted half note values. Level C might then interpret the foreground rhythm in terms of groups of three quarter notes each.

Level D is the skeletal bass motion. The dividing dominant splits the passage into two parts and reinforces the duple interpretation of the foreground rhythm already suggested by levels A and B. This interpretation clearly conflicts with the triple values of level C.

Schenker has provided an explanation for the choice of levels D, A, and B over level C as the preferred metric indicators of the passage. In his analysis of the C-minor fugue subject, he pointed out that the upper voice "is really a neighbor note motion signifying only a stationary tone, and against the motion of the middle voice it seems to fade in importance." The upper voice in the present case is also essentially stationary; hence a duple meter is likely to arise here from the interaction of the more structurally essential strata of the bass and inner voices (A, B, and D) and not from the triple grouping that is implied by the static, middleground pitch motion on level C.

The failure to distinguish significant middleground spans from essentially stationary tones has resulted in questionable kinds of rhythmic analyses. The best example of this is Rudolph Westphal's analysis (example 3.12) of the very same C-minor fugue about which Schenker made his point.[12]

Example 3.12

In A, Westphal pays far more attention to the highest voice in the

12. The example is from Westphal's *Allgemeine Theorie...*, p. 64.

passage and counts four beats, starting from the second *c* (these beats
are the chronos protos). The result is his strange accentual division
of the subject into two parts, shown in B. This division interrupts the
first third descent of the inner voice from *a-flat*; Westphal is apparently oblivious to this motion. Furthermore, he alters the traditional
notation in order to make his point. That grouping (in C) indicates
connecting beams on the notes marked by the asterisks. Rather than
being disjunct phrase endings, as indicated by Westphal, these tones
of the inner voice can be more easily seen to lead to one another
when they are conventionally beamed.

Paying more attention to the rate of recurrence of these middleground tones of the inner voice yields the following when the regularity of the motion is extended:

Example 3.13

The integration of this rhythmic stratum with other aspects of the
fugue becomes clear when it is recognized as being a literal augmentation of a foreground descent in the countersubject (in brackets in
example 3.14).

Example 3.14

Hence the inner voice motion of a middleground stratum becomes
duplicated in the foreground detail; and such a relationship becomes
a contributor to the compositional coherence of rhythmic and pitch
configurations because of the multiple appearances of these configurations on different levels.

The aspect of the analysis of rhythmic stratification that remains to be discussed in this chapter is the difference between rhythm-to-pitch and pitch-to-rhythm procedures. The kind of Schenkerian analysis that discovers middleground pitch designs on the basis of rules of voice-leading is representative of a pitch-to-rhythm approach. As indicated in example 3.8, a quarter note motion was discovered on the basis of a middleground arpeggiation, and a dotted half note motion was discovered on the basis of the repetition of that arpeggiation. Both of these pitch designs were seen to create middleground rhythm—even though the meter signature has to provide a performer with a clue to their discovery.

In spite of the necessary clue in the notation, these rhythmic strata are considered to be determined by pitch because pitch-to-rhythm analysis puts itself in the same position to the music as a listener who does not have the written score as a guide. In this sense, then, the triadic ascents of the middleground are rhythm-producing if they are apprehended, and a metric relationship may then emerge from the interaction of these middleground events with the foreground.

In view of this, the same must be true of the analysis of the C-minor fugue. Were the subject incorrectly considered by a listener to begin on a downbeat, for example, then the ensuing pitch recurrences of the pattern formed by the first three notes would tend to accentuate the upper voice and lead even further away from the structurally essential motion of the inner voice (example 3.15).

Example 3.15

The eighth rest at the beginning of the passage will therefore be posited by anyone who recognizes the most significant pitch motion of the middleground to have its point of beginning in the inner voice, and not in the upper voice.

Alternatively, a rhythm-to-pitch procedure will value pitches (in terms of their assignment to middleground strata) on the basis of recurrent rhythmic groups. If such an approach were to consider the recurrence of the patterns marked 'B' in example 3.15 as being more accentually significant than the recurrence of the patterns marked 'A,' then the pitch events that correspond to the beginnings of B-patterns would be assigned to a more significant pitch level.

Both of these procedures seem capable of indicating important rhythmic strata so long as they are kept separate when questions of the ultimate origins of strata arise. As mentioned earlier, to speak of elements of the same stratum as being both rhythm- and pitch-determined is to reason circularly. It is to say both that a rhythmic strong point is created by the location of an important pitch, and that the importance of the pitch is created by its location on a rhythmic strong point. The two approaches are similar in the sense that they discover the recurrences of events belonging to some particular class in each case. They differ in that rhythm-to-pitch analysis interprets pitches on the basis of repetitions of rhythmic patterns, while the pitch-to-rhythm analysis of tonal music is based on certain long-standing principles of tonality, such as the implications of triadic structures as they appear in the context of a rigorous pitch system.

In light of the extensive history of pitch analysis of tonal music, rhythm-to-pitch methodology would appear to be impoverished. In the following chapters, however, some basic rhythmic structures that arise from the interaction of pitch levels are investigated; and once those structures are examined, it may be possible to discover their appearance first within compositions and then to comment on the subsequent pitch designs they imply.[13]

13. A further aid to this approach is provided by the strata created by timbral, dynamic, and density events, which may interact with pitch strata created by recurrent rhythmic patterns.

4

Structures That Arise
from the Interaction
of Strata

In the preceding chapter, the analysis of the structure of musical rhythm has been approached in terms of a specific viewpoint. The rhythm of a musical work is first considered to be the summation of all its attacks: a resultant rhythm. Configurations on this foreground level may have structure in that they often consist of varied contours and varied intervals of time between attacks. Motion on this level is essentially uninterpreted, however, in that it is not characterized by accent or grouping. This is because any accents will divide a string of attacks into groups and will define a new rhythmic configuration. This configuration will be the motion from accent to accent; i.e., from the point of beginning of one group to the point of beginning of the next group. Moreover, this latter configuration will be included within the resultant rhythm of the piece; whatever rhythmic pattern it may form will be a constituent of the total pattern of attacks.

Similarly, this included level of motion from accent to accent, although it may function to interpret the foreground rhythm, cannot be itself interpreted or grouped without the postulation of some yet slower-moving configuration. In fact, any single level of motion remains uninterpreted so long as it is isolated from and unrelated to any other level of motion; the existence of accents necessarily implies the existence of another level of motion corresponding to the succession of the accents.

In terms of the above, the present chapter seeks to examine certain structures that arise from relationships various rhythmic levels in a composition may have to one another and to develop an analytic technique based on these relationships. The structures fall into two broad categories. The first is one in which the rate of any level of

motion in a piece can be expressed as a simple multiplication or
division (by an integer greater than 1) of the rate of any other level
of motion in the piece. The resulting structure of the interaction of
levels like these may be characterized, metaphorically, as *rhythmic
consonance*,

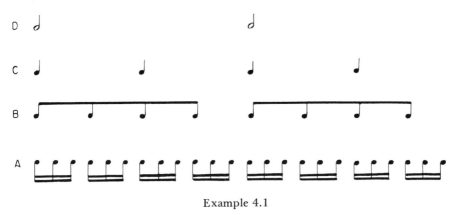

Example 4.1

Example 4.1 is a schematization of rhythmic consonance. Any of
its levels is a simple multiplication or division of any other of its
levels. Further, there is no one level of motion that can significantly
contradict an accentuation of the foreground based on some other
level of motion in the example. Thus if level C were considered to be
an important, meter-defining middleground motion, neither level B
nor level D would create a basis for objection. These alternative strata
provide, on the contrary, a reinforcement to such an interpretation
since there is a neat, vertical alignment of all the elements of all the
levels. This alignment is indicated by the essential structure of example 4.1: 2 against 4 against 8 against 24.

The second broad category under discussion extends the conven-
ient metaphor and may be characterized as *rhythmic dissonance*.
The simplest structure in this category is the simultaneous division
of a span of time into two and three equal segments. Any number of
additional possibilities will apply, however, so long as there are found
to be two levels in a piece that cannot be expressed as a simple multiplication or division of each other. Example 4.2 provides a sample
schematization of typically dissonant rhythmic relationships. Although levels C and D are consonant to each other, and levels B and

D are consonant, the same does not apply to B and C—nor to be sure, to any of the levels in terms of level A. The structure of example 4.2 shows these relationships clearly: 2 against 4 against 6 against 7.

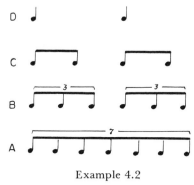

Example 4.2

It is important to stress that the structures being discussed here are the products of combining the attack patterns of two or more levels. These structures are the outcome of a further stage of analysis that must take place after the various individual levels of motion in a piece are postulated by the rhythm-producing criteria described in the preceding chapters. The ultimate combination of all the attack patterns of the various levels will, of course, restore the foreground (resultant) rhythm, but this is not the goal of this stage of analysis. The goal is, rather, to discover intermediate structures that have a controlling and interpretive function with respect to the foreground and that contribute to the aesthetic coherence of a composition by virtue of their repetition.

1. Rhythmic consonance

The opening eight bars of Mozart's *Eine Kleine Nachtmusik* (K.525) provide an example of rhythmic consonance that is accessible to either pitch-to-rhythm or rhythm-to-pitch analysis (example 4.3). Using the former methodology, the vital middleground motion is found first in the top violin part, an arpeggiated ascent from the first to the fifth scale step in m. 2. Measure 3 prolongs the fifth scale step (*d*) by supplying a *c*, initializing a descent of a third from *d*. This passing *c* is accompanied by its own bass note, provided on the third beat of m. 4. The completion of the descent of a third occurs

Example 4.3

in m. 5; the *b* is supplied by the first violin and doubled by the second violin. The essential motion of the first five measures is indicated in example 4.4: a motion to $\hat{5}$, and a descent of a third from $\hat{5}$.

Example 4.4

Example 4.4 also indicates the essential middleground motion of mm. 5–9. This motion remains in the second violin part and consists of a periodic prolongation of the *b* by means of its upper neighbor, *c*. In bar 10, the *c* becomes a passing tone, and the motion ascends back up to $\hat{5}$—this time accompanied by parallel motion in the bass.

Taking this essential middleground motion as a point of departure, the question of rhythm in this composition becomes an exploration of how the unique placement of middleground events gives rise to patterns that are integrated with the rest of the piece. Example 4.5 is a rhythmic stratification of the first eight measures. Level A begins with the effective foreground motion: a dotted rhythm which repeatedly divides the time span of four eighth notes into the attack pattern, 3 1. Supplying the mediating third of the tonic triad in m. 2 again produces the 3 1 pattern on level A. This motion is paralleled on level C (upper part of the staff), which is a representation of the rhythmic placement of only those middleground events discussed and graphed in example 4.4. On level C, these middleground events create a large dotted rhythm; they divide the time span of four half notes into a 3 1 attack pattern.

In the first four measures, then, there is a linkage of the rhythm of the middleground to the rhythm of foreground detail. The motion from $\hat{1}$ to $\hat{5}$ becomes one dotted rhythm, and the introduction of both the passing *c* and the bass tone (*d*) becomes a second one. Where level C takes note of only

Example 4.5

the first instance of the *g* in the first measure, level B presents the
rhythm of repetition of this pitch. Level D, on the other hand, is
reflexively determined and interprets the first two bars as I and the
second two bars as an auxiliary V^7. The rhythmic consonance of all

Example 4.5, continued

the levels is further enhanced by the literal augmentation of the motion of level A (3 1) that appears on level C.

The beginning of measure 5 introduces a striking new aspect to the relationships between the levels. Where the first four bars were characterized by a 3 1 pattern in the melody, m. 5 begins with a *g* that is repeated after a time span of only two eighth notes (see level A). This is accompanied by the introduction of the faster rates in the second violin, viola, and cello—all of which are rhythmically consonant. Comparing m. 5 with m. 1 is helpful here. In m. 1 all of the instruments divide a time span into 3 1; in m. 5 these same instruments divide the same time span in halves, in quarters, and in eighths.

The brilliance and rhythmic elegance of this piece can be seen by what happens on level C, beginning at m. 5. Just as the middleground events determined by example 4.4 first divided a span of four half notes into 3 1 on level C, they now divide that same span into 2 2, maintaining not only a rhythmic level that is consonant to the piece but also a linkage of the rhythm of the middleground with the rhythm of foreground detail.

Hence rhythmic consonance describes a general relationship, but each piece may make use of it in a unique manner. This particular piece is extraordinary not only because it links the middleground rhythm to the foreground motion but also because a significant change in the foreground motion (at m. 5) is accompanied by exactly the same change on the same middleground level: levels A and C begin with dotted values and then change simultaneously to equal values.

Several points need to be made about the above methodology. First, it is not an analysis of the rhythm of melody. Beginning at m. 5, the first violin is not the only voice that resolves the *c*. This resolution is also accomplished by the second violin, and the structurally essential motion remains with this instrument until the first violin (momentarily an inner voice) brings the line back from *b* up to *d* in bar 10.

Second, all rhythmic patterns of middleground levels are determined exclusively by pitch criteria. Significant pitches are chosen on the basis of principles of tonal structure, and then the rhythmic patterns formed by these pitches may be posited.

Finally, metric interpretation of the absolute surface motion of the piece is a function of the interaction of the levels. Note how the interaction of levels A, B, and D suggests a slow $\frac{4}{2}$ meter. Level B interprets the foreground in terms of a succession of half notes, and level D groups the half notes in repeating units of four. The only strong quarter note motion early in the piece occurs between the first two attacks in m. 5. Measure 9 is the first clear representation of the meter signature: the cello changes pitch at quarter note intervals.

A rhythm-to-pitch analysis of the same example yields similar results and has the added advantage here of enabling a comparison of rhythmic patterns on the uninterpreted foreground level. Considering first the determination of the principal rhythmic strata of the piece, the half note motion of level B (example 4.5) is a function of the recurrence of the 3 1 pattern within the first bar. The motion of level D is determined by the recurrence of the attack pattern formed in the first two bars.

The discovery of level C requires some exploration. The predominance of the dotted rhythms, on the extreme foreground, presents the analyst with an opportunity to seek an augmentation of the pattern on a slower level. In this instance, the results of such a search (the upper staff of level C) are fruitful, and thus the long dotted rhythm may be discovered by rhythm-to-pitch techniques. The more obvious motion on level C grows out of the rhythm of pattern-change in the first four measures. Hence the alternation of the rhythmic pattern of m. 1 with that of m. 2 gives rise to the whole note motion indicated on the lower part of the staff of level C. (Significantly, this motion is not accessible to pitch-to-rhythm analysis for the first four measures.)

The main characteristic of rhythm-to-pitch analysis is that the beginnings of repetitions of patterns become points of accent. These points of accent then call attention to the specific pitches which fall on them; on level A, for example, an extension of the dotted rhythm calls attention first to the *g* and then to the *b* in bar 2 and yields the arpeggiation of the tonic triad in that measure. In short, as has been said before, any configuration that is discovered on the basis of rhythm-to-pitch has to begin exclusively with rhythmic patterns before any evaluation of the structural function of pitches is considered.

On the uninterpreted level, rhythm-to-pitch procedure accounts for the more unique aspects of foreground rhythmic detail in this composition. Example 4.6 illustrates that the eighth note motion of measures 2 and 4 gives rise to the attack pattern, 3 1 1 1 1 1 in each case.

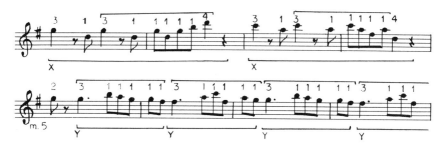

Example 4.6

This uninterpreted pattern continually reappears as a chain, beginning in m. 5. The structural identity of all the instances of this rhythmic pattern in example 4.6 is not immediately apparent. This is because the first appearances of the pattern (in bars 2 and 4) are subject to a different accentual interpretation than are those which follow them (the patterns marked 'Y').

As in chapter three, the choice of proper interpretation here again becomes a choice between different middleground strata; there is clearly no way to solve arguments exclusively in terms of an ambiguous foreground. This is precisely because such a foreground will be transformed in one or another way, depending upon the choice of accenting middlegrounds. The repetition of pattern in example 4.6, indicated by the Ys, strongly brings out an alternating motion between *g* and *f-sharp*. It is only when the principal metric accent is understood as the interaction of the foreground with the repeating patterns marked 'X' in the example, however, that the chain of Y patterns is seen to be displaced from the prevailing meter by a distance of a quarter note.

This displacement can be more easily seen if the Y patterns are shifted over onto the metric accent already established by the X patterns:

Example 4.7

The effect of this pattern shift does not alter the essential pitch structure of the piece. What it does is to place the harmonically functional *g* and *f-sharp* of the inner voice directly on the established metric strong points. Mozart's displacement of these patterns by one quarter note has the opposite effect. The metric strong points, created by former pattern repetitions, call attention not to the *g* and *f-sharp* of an inner voice but rather to the *b* and *c* of the second violin. In its original form, then, this composition does not run the risk of obscuring the structural tones of the second violin (in mm. 5–9) by accentuating the harmonically operative tones of the first violin (*g* and *f-sharp*). Rather, these latter tones—and their attendant patterns—are displaced and unaccented. They do not provide accents for grouping the foreground rhythm but appear, instead, in the context of the accentual groupings provided by the more structurally essential levels of middleground motion displayed in example 4.5.

The compositional coherence of rhythmic structure in this piece can be demonstrated by either of the above procedures. Rhythm-to-pitch analysis indicates the repetition of the 3 1 1 1 1 1 patterns on the uninterpreted level. The displacement of these patterns, indicated in example 4.6, illustrates that they are not a source of stress or accent interpretation, although they are a source of homogeneity of design when considered purely as attack patterns. Pitch-to-rhythm analysis indicates the simultaneous presence of the 3 1 pattern on the foreground and on a prominent middleground level—and the subsequent similar alteration of motion on both of these levels. Both procedures demonstrate the rhythmic consonance of all the levels. Significantly, the displaced chain of Y patterns in the example is able to play against the accent interpretation provided by the consonant rhythmic levels. This chain remains merely displaced, however. It is not rhythmically dissonant, since it does not introduce a consistently dissonant time-division into the piece.

As the piece progresses, Mozart continually exploits its consonant rhythmic levels. Some of these levels are allowed to surface momentarily to become the foreground rhythm. The content of m. 11 (example 4.8) is a good example of this; it brings level B to the surface.

Example 4.8

The dotted rhythm, which has appeared in the span of half a measure (in m. 1) and in the span of two measures (middleground of mm. 1 and 2), ultimately appears in the span of a single measure in bars 18 and 19. As has occurred on the other levels, this motion is immediately followed by equal divisions of the same time span (example 4.9).

Example 4.9

An equivalent dotted rhythm is generated by a density change in bar 28 (example 4.10).

Example 4.10

Ultimately, it can be said that rhythmic consonance between the levels of a piece makes it possible to populate those levels with similar patterns, as Mozart has done. Patterns, such as the dotted rhythms that appear on various levels in the preceding example, will differ in the rate of their progression, their individual tempo. Yet these differences of tempo will have a simple relationship to each other. In example 4.5 each increasingly reductive level halves the tempo of the immediately preceding level.

Furthermore, any rhythmic stratification that is characterized by multiple, consonant middleground levels will give rise to metric interaction between those levels. This is because such a structure satisfies the metric requirement of a slower regular rate within a faster one, and, again, consonant levels of motion are defined by this condition.

2. Rhythmic dissonance

To examine rhythmic dissonance, for which the above simple relationships no longer hold, the same methodology used to examine rhythmic consonance is applicable. First, the music is considered to be uninterpreted, then the various middleground levels are postulated, then the structures that are formed on or between the levels are examined, and finally the various middleground levels are evaluated to determine which of them has special relevance for a metric accentuation of the foreground rhythm.

In addition, an examination of rhythmic dissonance relates directly to questions and examples that have been posed earlier in this study—particularly to the problem of the compositional coherence of different rhythmic designs in a piece. The structures formed by dissonant rhythmic levels provide the keys to understanding how different designs may have a common source.

It is helpful to begin with a consideration of the simplest kind of dissonance, formed by a bipartite and tripartite division of the same time span. This is the basis of hemiola, which has been traditionally described as the relationship between two possible interpretations of six equidurational pulses (example 4.11). The six pulses in the example are indeed the raw material that will be divided into either two groups of 3 or three groups of 2, but there is nothing about these six pulses that describes a relationship between the alternate

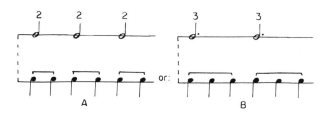

Example 4.11

divisions. This is because the divisions are not foreground phenomena. Rather, division A is a function of one middleground level, and division B is a function of another. The structure of hemiola must therefore be expressed as a relationship between two middleground levels (not between either of the middlegrounds and the foreground), and it takes the form of the combined attack patterns of the two levels (example 4.12).

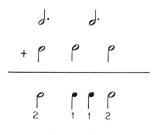

Example 4.12

As the above example indicates, a conflation of the two aspects of hemiola rhythm results in either the notated pattern, 𝅗𝅥 𝅘𝅥 𝅘𝅥 𝅗𝅥, or the attack-point pattern, 2 1 1 2. As a graphic description of structure, the numerical configuration is preferable because it is economical. It provides an unaccented pattern that is minimally necessary to indicate either of the middleground interpretations. In the form, 2 1 1 2, the pattern is uninterpreted. A bipartite interpretation may be indicated by a bar line or a slash: 2 1/1 2; and a tripartite division may be similarly indicated: 2/ 1 1/2. Thus the structure is a common source for either interpretation. Furthermore, the six pulses that are theoretically grouped by either interpretation are not lost in the pattern; they are the sum of its numerical values.

The numerical form of the structure is also preferable because it is general and useful as an analytic referent. First, it is applicable to any time span within which it may occur in a composition—regardless of how it may appear in music notation. It may therefore describe the structure of two dissonant middleground levels, one of which divides a time span of 6 measures in half and the other of which divides the same span in thirds.

Second, the numerical pattern establishes a basis for uncovering the compositional coherence of other accentual groupings, like the one just mentioned, even though these others may occupy different time spans. The formal structure of 2 against 3 will be the same in the span of one measure as it will be in the span of six measures—or half a measure. As such, the numerical form of this pattern is an aid to recognizing the condition of identity, on the uninterpreted level, that prevails between any of its occurrences in a composition, regardless of the accentuated musical form that the pattern may take (example 4.13).

Example 4.13

As mentioned previously, the formal identities indicated by the above example are often obscured by the tendency to ignore attack-point configurations and to concentrate exclusively on accentuated forms, in spite of the fact that both of these levels are relevant to and constituents of the structure of rhythm.

A manifestation of 2 against 3 between two middleground strata is illustrated by the opening bars of Chopin's Mazurka, Op. 59, no. 3 (example 4.14).

Example 4.14

The first two measures clearly divide into two by the registral alteration of the *f-sharp* in the bass—or the reduplication of the accompanimental pattern in the left hand (pitch-to-rhythm). Pitch-to-rhythm
analysis also finds that a middleground arpeggiation of the tonic
triad, *f-sharp–a–c-sharp*, divides the same two-measure span into
three equal parts. This latter observation provides a functional explanation for the double neighbor-note motion (*b-sharp* and *d*); this
motion delays the arrival of the fifth scale step until the second
beat of m. 2.

Example 4.15 indicates how 2   1 1 2 operates on the two-
measure span as a relationship between bass motion (3   3) and
middleground arpeggiation (2   2   2). The interaction of the two
levels of motion produces the intermediate pattern indicated in
parentheses.

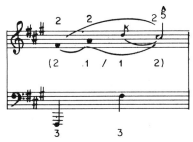

Example 4.15

This example also calls attention to the crucial placement of the
upper neighbor, *d*, which coincides with the bass motion and therefore lends impetus to the metric interpretation indicated by the
slash.

The mazurka also provides a good example of a nested structure.
Three against two operates between two middleground strata, as
described, but it also appears as a more foreground feature by attack-point criterion. The first measure sets off the three attack
points of the left hand (2 2 2) against the slower time interval
between *f-sharp* and *g-sharp* in the right hand (3   1). The nesting
of this pattern within the structure of the longer span is indicated,
again in parentheses, in m. 1 of example 4.16.

The presence of the nested structure requires an underscoring
of the theoretical principles involved. By different sets of criteria,

identical instances of an uninterpreted rhythm structure
(2   1   1   2) are formed. Each may be considered to be a
rhythmic sub-pattern of the piece, except that the structure con-

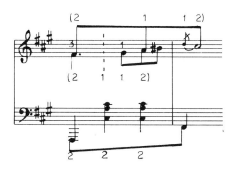

Example 4.16

tained in the first measure is a product of foreground, note-to-
note motion while the arpeggiation of the F-sharp minor triad is
a middleground motion for which each significant note is considered to be prolonged until the next note of equivalent significance
is sounded. Thus the 2   1 1 2 structure is descriptive of four
levels of stratification and establishes a formal identity between the
levels when they are taken as pairs.

As mentioned earlier in this chapter, this structure is intermediate;
it is neither the complete foreground rhythm nor any single level of
motion. Rather, uninterpreted structures like 2   1 1 2 are static
representation of what may often be conflicting rates of motion in a
piece. They provide a language with which to relate dissonant strata
to each other in order to establish a basis for describing the homogeneity of rhythmic design in a composition. (In this context, note
also the change from eighth-note duplets to triplets in m. 2 of example 4.14).

The above paragraph has indicated that a structure may describe
conflicting rates of motion. Example 4.17 provides two instances
that dramatically represent this phenomenon. In A the duple motion
of the melodic line forms 2   1 1 2 with the bass motion; in B the
triple motion of the melodic line is dissonant with the duple motion
of the bass. Since the pitch function of the bass takes precedence in
either case, accent interpretations for A and B are 2/ 1 1/2 and

2 1/ 1 2 respectively. Note how no amount of dynamic stress on the
d-flat of A (bar 1) or the *d-sharp* of B (bar 1) will change the accentuation, which is determined by a middleground pitch stratum in
each case—and not by a dynamic level.

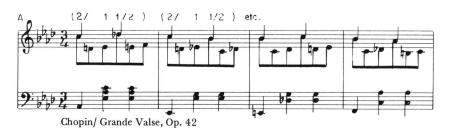

Chopin/ Grande Valse, Op. 42

Example 4.17

Yet the use of 2 1 1 2 as a structure may be extended beyond
the description of simultaneously conflicting rates. As an analytic
referent, the structure may stand for the progressive use of two
mutually dissonant rates of motion as a composition develops. Example 4.18 demonstrates a typical application of this principle. The
essential middleground motion of example 4.18 is indicated arhyth-
mically in example 4.19. First, there is an ascent to $\hat{3}$, incorporating
a voice exchange between the treble and the bass. Because of this,
$\hat{3}$ is implicit on the first beat. Next, there is an intervening upper
neighbor that prolongs and then returns to the third scale step. This
is followed by a descent to $\hat{2}$ over a dividing dominant. In the fifth
measure, the descent of a third is completed; but the *b* returns, and
it appears that the structurally operative tone is still $\hat{3}$ (see the dotted
slur in example 4.19). From m. 6 to the end of the passage, the motion is identical to what has come before, except that now there is

no reiterated *b* in m. 8, and the middleground upper voice descends from *b* to *g*: $\hat{3}$-$\hat{2}$-$\hat{1}$.

This middleground motion is shown below in example 4.18. In the first four measures, a significant middleground event occurs once at the beginning of every measure. Bar one sounds the tonic. The total foreground content of the bar establishes $\hat{3}$, which forms a tenth with the bass. Bar two begins with the upper neighbor; the tenth between treble and bass is retained. In bar three, the return to the third scale step is the beginning event, accompanied again by the

Mozart/ K.525/Minuet

Example 4.18

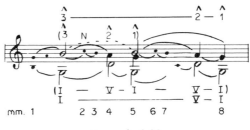

Example 4.19

lower tenth. The V^6 of V at the end of the bar is rhetorical and should not appear on the structural level being described. The real arrival on *a* is implied at the beginning of bar 4, where there is a structural support in the form of a dividing dominant.

As previously mentioned, bars 5–8 repeat the above motion, except that the rhythm of the same middleground events has now changed. Instead of one event for every three quarter notes, the return from the upper neighbor and the subsequent descent to $\hat{1}$ establishes a half-note motion. Thus the attack pattern of middleground events in example 4.18 changes at m. 6 from 3 3 to 2 2 2; the former pattern groups the foreground quarter notes in threes, while the latter groups them in twos. In this case, 2   1 1 2 may be said to be compositionally exploited in the horizontal sense, as a succession from one of its accent interpretations to another one.

The pattern, 2   1 1 2 can be descriptive of simultaneous and different rates in this example, however, if the accentuation of the first four measures is considered to extend through the next four. If a $\frac{3}{4}$ meter is thus conceptually maintained, then the middleground events in mm. 6–7 form a 2   1 1 2 pattern with the conceptual points of accent. This is shown in example 4.20, where the lower line is conceptually supplied on the basis of the first four bars of the passage.

Mozart's rhythmic manipulation of identical sets of middleground pitch events would not be of especial interest here were it not inte-

Example 4.20

grated, as well, with the rest of the movement. In example 4.21, the attack-point intervals within the upper line of each measure set off the duple bar divisions of the upper line against the repeated melodic thirds of the accompaniment, and this scheme continues, as indicated in example 4.22, when the lower neighbor-note motion is understood as prolonging the first note of the bar.[1]

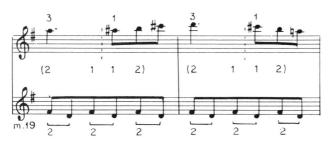

Example 4.21

Example 4.22

The movement is thus seen to employ 2   1 1 2 as a structure, first as the interaction of different middleground levels of motion in the context of a span of two measures, and then on a more foreground level in the context of a span of one measure.

One final aspect of this kind of rhythmic structure remains to be discussed: the prevalence of a pattern such as 2   1 1 2 as a fore-

1. This is only one way of interpreting the first bar of example 4.22. It can just as easily be read as a consonant level of motion determined by the repetition of the *g*:

ground attack pattern, regardless of whether or not it represents two conflicting rates of motion between deeper levels. A typical instance of this is illustrated by the fifth Diabelli Variation (example 4.23). The second and third measures of the example create a level of motion that is dissonant with the established meter. The sforzando markings clearly divide the time span into three half-note beats, and this stratum forms 2   1 1 2 when combined with the principal metric accent. In the span of two measures, the pattern is thus representative of conflicting rates of motion. This is not the case, however when the structure appears on the foreground in the second and fourth bars of the example. These latter statements of the structure are not conflicting rates of motion (no parentheses in the sketch), but neither are they disinterested foreground motives. Indeed, they repeat, on the foreground, the same attack pattern that is formed by the interaction of the sforzando attacks with the metric accent; and as such they are integrated with the structure formed between two deeper rhythmic levels of the piece.[2]

Beethoven/ Op. 120, Var. 5

Example 4.23

A similar example is provided by Chopin (example 4.24). Here the pattern recurrence within the first two bars divides that time span in half. The following two bars trisect the same time span with stresses, forming 2   1 1 2 with the previously established accentual scheme (shown in parentheses above the large bracket). The nested form of the structure, in bar 3, is heavily exploited as the composition pro-

2. It is interesting that Riepel's improvement of his student's composition (example 1.3) consisted to a large degree in the introduction of the same pattern (2 1 1 2) as a repeated foreground configuration.

gresses and is shown without parentheses below the small bracket.

Chopin/ Op. 18

Example 4.24

Chopin's waltzes are a veritable lexicon of ways in which this structure is utilized compositionally. Bar 16 of opus 18 displays the pattern in another light (example 4.25). The measure's division by the first attack-point interval in the right hand (3 1) forms a 2   1 1 2 sub-pattern with the three attacks of the bass. Measures

Example 4.25

86–87 of the same piece use dynamics to group the foreground quarter notes in threes, while the pitch alternations of the right hand group the quarter notes in twos (example 4.26). This latter tripartite

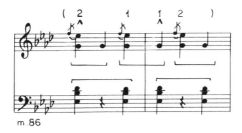

Example 4.26

division of the two-measure span is also a function of density recurrence in the right hand. At m. 122, yet another form of the structure
appears. This time the pattern is the total foreground rhythm, created by the resultant of the left and right hand attacks (example
4.27).

Example 4.27

The Valse Brillante, opus 34, no. 1, repeats the use of the structure
at the beginning (example 4.28, A), but transforms it in a later
section (example 4.28, B). In B 2   1 1 2 is a prominent sub-pattern
of the bar—with an included diminution of the dotted pattern (♩. ♪)
at the end of the bar (♩. ♩) .

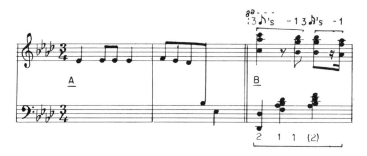

Example 4.28

In opus 34, no. 3, the structure emerges in two guises at m. 17 as a
result of recurrences of pitch patterns (example 4.29). The internal
groupings of the foreground, according to repetition of pitch and
contour, are indicated by brackets above and below the example.
The levels of motion created by these groupings are indicated in the

stratification above the example. Level A is the level of recurrence of descending four-note patterns, level B is the recurrence of the accompanimental pattern in the left hand, level C records the level of motion of the larger pattern that is repeated, and level D is the consonant division of the four bars into two groups of two. (This pairing of measures is established by pattern recurrence in the first 16 bars of the piece.)

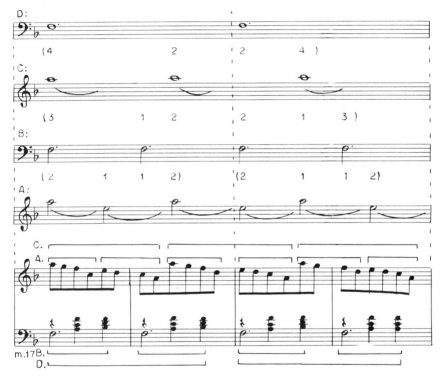

Example 4.29

The structures that arise from the interaction of strata are indicated between the levels of example 4.29, in parentheses. Between C and D there is a long 2 against 3 in the span of four measures. Between A and B there are two instances of 2 against 3, each of which fills out the span of 2 measures. The pattern formed between levels B and C is 3 against 4 (3 1 2 2 1 3); this is the true nexus structure of the example. On the one hand it contains the longer-valued

instance of 2 against 3 (4 2 2 4), and on the other hand it is contained by the two shorter-valued instances of the structure
(2   1 1 2/2   1 1 2).[3]

Another waltz, opus 64, no. 1 (example 4.30), makes a similar
use of pattern recurrence. Here again the accompanimental pattern
recurrence of level B is dissonant with the pattern recurrence on
level A. The bass arpeggiation (*d-flat* to *f*) of level B is the vital
middleground pitch motion, and thus the rate of progression of
events on this level is the operative meter-defining motion, producing the accentual interpretation of the pattern: 2   1/1 2. The
motion in bar 9 of the same waltz (see example 4.30) presents this
same attack structure as the interaction of the bass attacks with the
slower time interval between the *b-flat* and *a-flat* of the upper line.

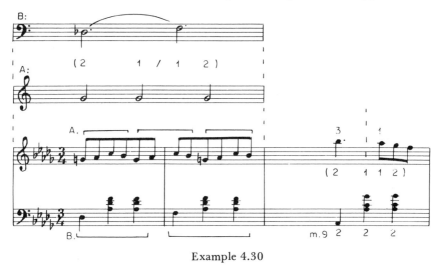

Example 4.30

3. The aesthetic function of intermediate structures

The point of this discussion of Chopin's waltzes is not to suggest
that they are all, somehow, the same, nor is it to reduce all of
rhythm to a single structure. Rather each composition is rhythmically stratified in its own unique way; deeper levels of motions are
sometimes consonant and sometimes dissonant with each other. Although the most common dissonant relationship forms a 2 1 1 2

3. The kinds of relationships discussed in this paragraph are examined more closely in
chapter 5.

structure, it must be stressed that the rhythmic levels of each composition are created by unique pitch events. Furthermore the succession from structure to structure (whether 2   1 1 2 appears in
the span of one bar or two bars or as the foreground detail, *and*
the order in which the various statements of the structure appear)
is also unique for each compostion.

The ultimate aspect of the unique differentiation of these structures in a composition is their accentual interpretation. As accentuated patterns, 2   1/1 2 and 2/ 1 1/2 have very different
meanings, as indicated by the previous examples—particularly
example 4.17, A and B. The reason for the present kind of analysis
now becomes more obvious. The accentuation, pitch parentage,
time span, depth of level, and succession of dissonant and consonant structures in compositions are in each case uniquely combined, but the aesthetic coherence of the rhythmic designs of each
composition is made visible by the consistent appearance of uninterpreted sub-patterns, like 2   1 1 2, between the various levels
and as an integrated foreground detail. By demonstrating how a
composition generates and places and interprets these intermediate
structures, an analysis describes rhythmic differentiation. But by
indicating the prevalence of and the identities between the structures, an analysis uncovers a homogeneity of rhythmic design within
the same composition.

This dual process can be seen more clearly in a specific example.
Mozart's Sonata K. 332 begins with an accentual interpretation,
provided by middleground pitch events, that represents the time
signature (example 4.31). Measure 1 begins on $\hat{1}$, m. 2 is an ascent

Example 4.31

to $\hat{5}$, m. 3 is the beginning of a descent of a fifth from $\hat{5}$, and m. 4 prolongs the *b-flat* of m. 3 by supporting it with a significant, passing dominant harmony. The foreground detail of bars 3 and 4 introduces a 2   1 1 2 structure as the durations of the final four melodic notes.

The next four measures continue the rate of progression of the middleground descent (example 4.32). The *b-flat* ($\hat{4}$) is resolved to an *a* ($\hat{3}$) in the left hand of m. 5; the *g* ($\hat{2}$) appears at the beginning of m. 6. Bar 7 is the arrival on $\hat{1}$ and the beginning of a motion back up to $\hat{3}$ via the *g* in m. 8. Rhythmically, however, there is a level of half-note motion created by the contour repetition of the descending intervals in mm. 5–6 (see the brackets in example 4.32). This repetition of descending intervals segments mm. 5–6 into three equal parts. The imitation in the left hand in mm. 7–8 has the same effect. Note also how these trisections of the two-measure spans are enhanced by the held, dotted quarter notes in each case. The half-note motion formed by these trisections creates a 2   1 1 2 structure in each of the two-measure spans when combined with the rate of recurrence of middleground events. The structure also reappears closer to the foreground as the embellishing inner voice of m. 8.

Example 4.32

All of this sonata will not be duplicated here. The reader is asked to observe that mm. 9–10 restore $\hat{5}$ via the upper neighbor, *d*. The upper line then passes through *b-flat* and returns to *a*; mm. 11–12 continue the regular rate of middleground progression by descending from $\hat{2}$ to $\hat{1}$. Following this mm. 13–21 repeat the middleground motion of the first 12 bars—a descent of a fifth from $\hat{5}$, a return to $\hat{3}$, and a final descent to $\hat{1}$. The rhythmic levels of this section, however, are fully consonant with each other, as they are in mm. 1–4.

At mm. 23–24 radically new rhythmic designs appear (example 4.33). Again, however, their essential structure is well integrated with previous structures in the piece. The middleground arpeggiation of the D-minor triad in the upper voice has a 2 1 1 2 attack pattern (see level A). Furthermore, within m. 23 the upper attack interval between *d* and *f* forms the same structure when combined with the previously established quarter-note motion of the principal metric scheme. In addition, Mozart clearly indicates, through quality of attack, a similar bisection of m. 24 by the staccato high *a*, followed by the slurred, three eighth notes of the descending triad. This again forms 2 1 1 2 with the established metric accent. Note also an additional nested appearance of the structure on the foreground (indicated by the bracket).

Example 4.33

The next two measures exploit the bisection of a one-measure span by means of the time interval between the held attack and the sixteenth-note run in the right hand (example 4.34).

Example 4.34

The thematic material that follows in the dominant key again makes use of either consonant or well-integrated dissonant structures, as indicated in example 4.35.

Example 4.35

At m. 49, the varied repetition of the second theme, the dissonant structures take yet another form (example 4.36) as the interaction of two faster levels of motion. This faster configuration again generates a 2   1   1   2 pattern:

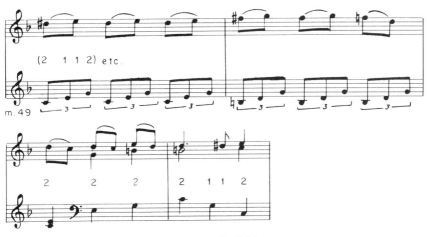

Example 4.36

Finally, the structure is artfully enclosed within a rhythmic inter-action of the right and left hands (example 4.37). Here the rate of change of dynamic level helps to accentuate the quarter-note motion of the left hand, while the eighth rest in the right hand detaches the final three attacks from the first half of the measure.

Example 4.37

This analysis does not exhaust the overall rhythmic detail of the sonata's exposition. It does indicate, however, the manner in which the rhythmic variety of the piece is controlled and unified by co-herent intermediate structures that arise from the interaction of middleground strata. Further, it provides a basis for understanding the metric accentuation of the piece as being determined by a pre-ferred middleground level—preferred because it carries the structurally most essential pitch events (as shown in examples 4.31 and 4.32).

The concentration on $\frac{3}{4}$ time in this chapter is not meant to suggest that dissonant structures appear in triple time only. In fact, the analysis of the $\frac{4}{4}$ exercise in chapter 3 (example 3.11) can now be completed (example 4.38). Here, the inner voice that parallels the middleground descent of a third from *g* creates a half-note motion;

Example 4.38

the six quarter notes of the foreground are grouped in pairs (see level B). At the same time, the upper voice rests on *c* for three beats and then prolongs the upper neighbor *d* for another three beats (see level C). Hence the interaction of these two levels forms a 2   1 1 2 pattern (indicated in parentheses). As mentioned before, the half-note motion is more vital because it is consonant with the bisection of the two measures provided by the essential motion from I to V and because the upper voice signifies merely a stationary tone. This observation gives rise, in turn, to the accent interpretation of the 2   1 1 2 pattern indicated in the example by the slashes.

4. Dual interpretation of dissonant structures

Structures formed by the interaction of dissonant strata are not always easily interpreted according to accent. When a situation arises in which either of the constituent levels of motion creating the dissonance may easily be the principal metric indicator, the result is syncopation.

The third movement of Mozart's G-minor Symphony, K. 550, illustrates this nicely. The six bars of example 4.39 are analyzed first in the arhythmic sketch of example 4.40.[4] Looking first at the most prominent long-term events, the passage is essentially a slow motion from $\hat{1}$ to $\hat{3}$ of a *g-minor* triad (indicated by half notes in example 4.40). This motion occurs over an equally important bass arpeggiation of the tonic triad (also indicated in half notes in the sketch).

Next, each arrival on a scale step is accompanied by a leap to an upper third and a descent through a third back to the scale step. In the sketch, $\hat{1}$ is immediately followed by a skip to *b-flat* and a descent through the interval of a third outlined by the skip. The *b-flat* is represented by a large quarter note, and the elements of the unfolding interval are designated by small quarter notes. The ensuing motion from $\hat{3}$ and subsequent return to $\hat{3}$ are identically graphed. Both of these spans of a third are indicated under brackets in the sketch. Note also that the passing tones in each of these unfolding thirds (*a* in the first; *c* in the second) are each supported by an auxiliary V harmony in the bass.

Finally, each of these passing tones just mentioned is itself prolonged by a descent through a third. This is indicated by the slurs under the isolated noteheads in the sketch. The diagram thus indicates three major levels: 1) the motion from $\hat{1}$ to $\hat{3}$, to which is attached 2) the unfolding thirds indicated by brackets, and 3) the smaller descents through a third that are attached to each passing tone of level 2.

The problem for accent interpretation of this passage is that the bracketed thirds in the sketch and the bass arpeggiations below them both comprise significant and purposeful motion. This is not a case where one of the levels is merely a neighbor-note motion, signifying only a stationary tone.

Looking now at the placement of these events in example 4.39, the rhythmic problem becomes more visible. On level A, the bass motion establishes a regular, dotted half-note stratum. This is under-

4. Schenker's analysis of this piece can be found in *Meisterwerke*, 2 (1926), p. 145, and my reading of the example concurs with his.

Example 4.39

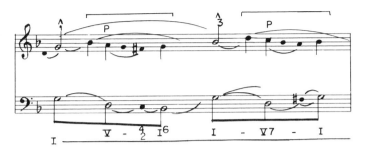

Example 4.40

scored by the inner voices, played by oboe and clarinet and indicated on level A'. Level B displays the rate of events shown under brackets in example 4.40. These establish a half-note motion that is dissonant with level A. Level C is the large-scale motion from $\hat{1}$ to $\hat{3}$, and it clearly bisects the passage.

The structure formed between levels A and B is indicated in parentheses: (2   1 1 2). If level A is the metric definer, then the accentuation of the structure must be 2 1/1 2; if level B is the metric definer, then the accentuation must be 2/ 1 1/2. Although it has been determined that events on both A and B are significant, a double accentuation of the rhythmic structure will not accomplish anything. The form 2/ 1/ 1/ 2 is no different from the uninterpreted form (2 1 1 2) because the effect of double accentuation is to eliminate all grouping within the structure.

Furthermore, bringing out both levels of motion with dynamic stresses will also accomplish nothing. Combining 2̌ 1 1̌ 2 with 2̌ 1̌ 1 2̌ creates 2̌ 1̌ 1̌ 2̌, which again is no different from the originally uninterpreted dissonant structure because it is undifferentiated and merely makes all of the attacks louder.

If the passage is to receive a single metric interpretation, the only solution is to designate one of the levels of motion as being the controlling metric indicator, while designating the other as being a significant, alternate level of motion that is strongly superimposed on the former one, and this is the meaning of syncopation. The two possibilities of the passage in question are shown in example 4.41.

> >   >   >   >
2 1/ 1 2   or   2/ 1 1/ 2
       A   B

Example 4.41

In A the meter is a function of the bass motion while the dissonant middleground motion superimposed by the upper voice is indicated by stresses. In B the meter is drawn from the upper voice, and the superimposed level of motion is in the bass, indicated by stresses. Note how level C (example 4.39) is of no help in making a choice between the two accentuations since it merely divides the passage into two instances of the same problem. Note also that the graphic use of dynamic markings to indicate a superimposed level of motion (in example 4.41) does not mean that this motion is necessarily created by stresses. To the contrary, the syncopation of this example is pitch-structural and emerges from a conflict between the motion of two vital middleground pitch configurations.

Of the two, the bass arpeggiation is the more influential, and the present analysis opts for 4.41, A as the essential rhythmic structure of the passage. This choice is based on the significant dividing dominants in the bass (shown below the staff in example 4.40). As a result of the placement of these bass events, the *b-flat* to *a* motion in m. 2 becomes a 6-5 suspension; similarly, the *d* to *c* in m. 5 is an 8-7 motion. (See this in example 4.39). Clearly then, the functions of the bass tones provide a context in which the events of the upper voice appear. And since they control the pitch context of the upper voice, they likewise provide a rhythmic context.

The ultimate conclusion of the above analysis is an underscoring of the implications of pitch-to-rhythm methodology: namely, that metric strong points do not come into being simply because a time signature is written on paper (just the opposite, in fact), nor is syncopation a stress on a "weak" beat—especially when the weakness of that beat is defined merely by a written time signature. Rather, syncopation has its source here in the structure of conflicting rates of motion, and in tonal music these rates may have as their ultimate sources individual pitch strata that are created by the variegated functions of pitches.

Syncopation may also be created by a consonant stratum of motion that is displaced from an established metric scheme. In example 4.42, the suspension formed by the tied eighth notes in m. 9 would seem to initiate a division of the bar into three equal segments. This level of motion would be dissonant with the metric bisections of the measure (3 3) that control this piece. These bisections can be seen in the two final bars of the example. The penultimate bar is divided by a dominant; the following bar is bisected by the lower-octave recurrence of the *d* as the functional register of the bass note.

Rather than continuing a triple division of the bar, however, the initial tied eighth-note suspension in m. 9 is soon followed by others that recur at intervals of time equal to three eighth notes (3 3), and this is not a dissonant time division. It is a consonant level of motion that is initially displaced from the beginning of m. 9 by a distance of a quarter note (see level A). Hence, although it initially begins with a dissonant time interval (a quarter note), the syncopation that is formed between (1) the previously established metric strong points, and (2) the level of motion of the tied eighth notes, is, in this case, not really the result of a superimposed dissonant stratum. It is, instead, the outgrowth of a displaced consonant stratum.

Bach/ Gigue for solo 'cello

Example 4.42

This displaced consonant stratum is, in fact, a part of a more general structure. Note how the displaced chain of tied eighth notes in the above example (level A) ultimately connects with the initial upbeat. The function of the upbeat now becomes realized as the true beginning of the displaced, consonant level of motion. (Figure 4.1 is a schematic illustration of this, as it appears in example 4.42.)

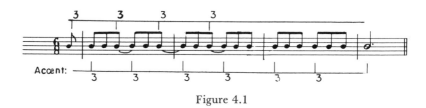

Figure 4.1

All upbeats serve this same essential function. They begin a consonant but displaced level of motion, even before the true beginning
accent is sounded (as in figs. 4.2 and 4.3). The consequent uninterpreted motion from upbeat to upbeat in the music will always make
a piece appear to be just a little ahead of itself, since the recurrences
of upbeats will always happen immediately before the recurrences of
more essential accentual points that are usually determined by significant, middleground pitch events.

Figure 4.2

Figure 4.3

The presence of such an upbeat scheme in a composition makes it
very easy for a composer to create syncopation with displaced consonance; he need only dynamically stress the chain of upbeats. Chopin does this most often in his mazurkas, as illustrated in example
2.12. Bach creates the syncopation in example 4.42 by using ties
to eliminate momentarily the attacks within the chain of recurring
accents, thus allowing the superimposed, displaced chain that begins
with the upbeat to dominate the attack rhythm of the music.

This chapter's discussion of dissonant strata and the various possibilities of accent interpretation may now be summarized by the following five examples. In example 4.43 the recurrence of the pattern indicated by the brackets establishes the quarter-note motion of level A (4 4 4). This is a simple middleground level and signifies a static *c*.

Example 4.43

In example 4.44 the same essential structure is presented, but the stressed events that give rise to level B are displaced by a sixteenth note from the motion of level A. The faster motion of level B (2 2 2) is consonant, however, with the time-divisions of level A (4 4 4), and so syncopation is created here by a displaced, consonant level of motion. The interaction of A and B forms 1 2̌ 1̌/1 2̌ 1̌/1 2̌ 1̌; the slashes are placed to conform with the controlling middleground pitch motion, which remains the repeated and essentially static *c* of level A.

Example 4.44

Example 4.45 introduces a true dissonant relationship. The four-note descending contours are still present in the music (above the

brackets), but the time signature is an instruction to read the middleground differently. Now there are four middleground events on level
A: (1) the c: (2 & 3) the motion of an inner voice upwards from g;
and finally (4) a downward step in the upper voice from c to b. Because the foreground pitches are grouped in threes by middleground
pitch events, the leading tone b in m. 2 is reflexively supported by
the final g of the measure. Compared to this motion, the essentially
static c on level B commands less attention, and so the interaction
of the two levels (3 against 4) is interpreted to conform with level
B: 3/ 1 2/2 1/3.

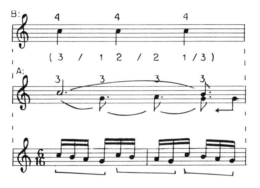

Example 4.45

It should be stressed that this interpretation recognizes level B as
a latent but unaccented level of motion. The music in this example is
shaped by the interaction of its unaccentuated contours with the
accenting middleground events of level A.[5] This is thus an example
of two mutually dissonant middlegrounds (A and B), one of which
provides interpretive accents because its pitch motions are of singular
significance to the tonal structure. There is, therefore, no syncopation in the example because the unaccented elements of level B do
not intrude.

5. Again it should be emphasized that the meter signature has not somehow created the
middleground pitch configuration of this example. Rather, the time signature is chosen from
among other possibilities in order to communicate graphically the prior, middleground
structure of the music, the rhythm of which is the true metric indicator. The ultimate study
of how this middleground is perceived by a listener must begin with developmental psychology, unless it is to be believed that this kind of perceptual act is somehow innate. It would
appear more likely that the ability to understand middleground levels is learned and developed until it becomes second nature to one who has gained the skill.

This fact is altered in example 4.46. Here the middleground interpretation remains the same on level A. The dissonant motion of level B, latent in example 4.45, is now brought out by stresses in example 4.46. This strong superimposition of a dissonant rate, and the subsequent syncopation between the levels, is indicated by stresses: 3́/ 1 2́/2 1́/3. Note that the controlling division of the foreground, indicated by slashes, is still provided by level A and that the stresses of level B (and the descending, four-note patterns they call attention to) play against the essential accent interpretation created by significant pitch motion.

Example 4.46

Example 4.47 reverses the roles of levels A and B. The time signature is now an instruction to read the events on Level B as the

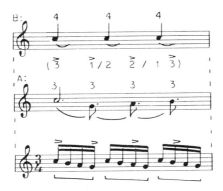

Example 4.47

primary middleground motion: an essentially static *c*. The pitches
of level A that are brought out by the stresses in the example are
now a subsidiary motion of an inner voice, and there is no longer a
stepwise motion from *c* down to *b* at the end of the passage. Hence
level B now controls the accentual division of the foreground, and
level A is a superimposed, dissonant rate created by dynamics. The
subsequent syncopation (that of a ragtime waltz) is indicated by an
alteration of the intermediate structure (in parentheses) appropriate
to the changed relationships in the example: 3 1/ 2 2/ 1 3.

The final possibility, not included here, is one of a conflict between two equally purposeful, middleground pitch motions, and
this problem has already been discussed in the analysis of Mozart's
G-minor Symphony K. 550 (examples 4.39 and 4.40). The result,
in such a case, may be the presence of purely pitch-structural syncopation.

The structures that arise from the interaction of strata are numerous and are not always as simple as those discussed in this chapter. Chapter 5 presents a more systematic exploration of structures
that evidence greater complexity.

5

Abstract Inclusion
Relationships

Any piece of music that makes extensive use of rhythmic structures characterized by equal time divisions at various levels will display certain formal relationships. This chapter will investigate those relationships in a manner that is directed towards their specifically musical aspects.

Clearly, the structures formed by the interaction of consonant and dissonant strata, such as those described in chapter 4, do not represent the total universe of rhythmic designs, but they do appear frequently in music. This present chapter is therefore minimal in the sense that it pertains to a limited aspect of rhythm and not to its universal foundation.[1]

1. The numerical display of structures

The attack-point technique described in chapter 2 is used here to display rhythmic configurations. In example 5.1, A and B, the placement of each number corresponds to a moment of attack. The value of each number is the amount of time until the next attack. This value may stand for the number of eighth, quarter, sixteenth notes,

---

1. A theory of rhythm that does consider the resultants of different divisions of the same time span to be the ultimate source of rhythmic structure has, in fact, been proposed by Joseph Schillinger in his book *The Schillinger System of Musical Composition* (New York, 1946). Schillinger opined that all foreground rhythm can be explained as either the resultants of dissonant time divisions or aggregates of segments of these resultants. The absurdity of the claim is obvious. One need only write a composition that uses one of these resultants and then invert the order of some of the note values; the rhythmic structure can be easily made to conform to no recognizable resultant. This argument (and other refutations of Schillinger) is put forth by John Backus in "Pseudo-Science and Music," *JMT* 4, no. 2 (1960), pp. 221–232. To reject resultants of dissonant time divisions altogether, simply because they are not the sum total of all of rhythm, however, would be unduly to disregard their significance. At deeper rhythmic levels these structures often appear, and their integration with certain aspects of foreground rhythm has been documented in chapter 4 of this study.

etc., until the next attack; or it may be considered the numerator of the fraction of time it represents. The denominator of this fraction is the sum of all the numerical values that make up the pattern.

$$
\begin{array}{lccccccc}
\text{A:} & 3 & & 1 & 2 & 2 & 1 & 3 \\
\text{B:} & 2 & 2 & 2 & 2 & & &
\end{array}
$$

Example 5.1

If all of 5.1, B were to occur in one second, for instance, then each 2 would signify 2/8 (or 1/4) of a second of time until the next attack. Similarly, in A each 2 would indicate 2/12 (or 1/6) of a second. Multiplying this hypothetical one second by any number makes the fraction apply in the same way to the product. Hence if all of B were to fill a span of ten seconds, each 2 would represent 2/8 (or 1/4) of ten seconds, and so forth for any span of real time.

Graphically, the structure is displayed to show this time relationship. Each number on the page is followed by an amount of blank spaces equal to the number. Thus in 5.1, A, 3 is followed by three blanks, 1 by one blank, 2 by two blanks, etc.

2. Consonant inclusion

The formal requirement for consonance between levels has already been described in chapter 4. The time value of each element of one level must be a simple multiplication or division (by an integer greater than 1) of the time value of any element of any other level. The resultant rhythm of any two or more interacting consonant levels will therefore be the attack pattern of the fastest level; i.e., this level *includes* the attacks of the slower levels.

In example 5.2 (2 against 4 against 8), the same time span is divided three ways.[2] Level A is a sequence of 8

2. The graphic spacing of levels B and C in this example has been altered to show the vertical alignment of attacks.

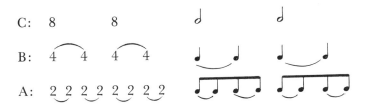

Example 5.2

equidurational attacks, B consists of 4 of such attacks, and C contains 2. The resulting rhythm is that of level A.

The inclusion of the slower-moving levels within the faster ones can be shown by grouping the time values of the faster levels. Hence adding the time values of level A in pairs (indicated by slurs) produces level B; doing the same in B produces C, and adding the elements of level A in groups of four produces level C. This summation of values is the effect of tying noteheads in the corresponding music notation of the example.

3. Resultants of dissonant levels

When two levels dissonant to each other interact, each pattern contributes its attacks to the gross rhythmic pattern created by the combination. Either level of motion can be isolated, however, by summing the numerical values of the resultant pattern to equal, in each case, the number which represents the other time division that contributes to the pattern.

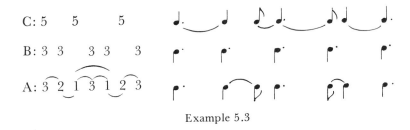

Example 5.3

Example 5.3, A is the pattern formed by 3 against 5. Summing the attacks of this resultant pattern to equal 3 in each case (lower slurs) will produce the placement of attacks indicated on level B—which is the division of the time span into five equal segments. Summing the values of the resultant pattern to 5 in each case (upper slurs) will isolate the moments of attack of level C—the trisection of the time span.[3]

It should be recognized that the placement of slashes (symbolizing bar lines) that the previous chapter has used for these dissonant structures is based on the above technique of summing. Thus in example 5.4, A (3 against 4), the controlling meter is indicated by the quadruple time division of level B (summing the values of level A to 3), and the superimposed level of syncopation (level C) is a triple time division that is isolated by summing the values of level A to 4.

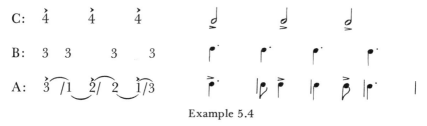

Example 5.4

This structure, and the others discussed in this section, can therefore be viewed from either end. Either level A (example 5.4) can be derived from combining levels B and C, or levels B and C can be derived from two different summations of the time values of level A.

4. Prime dissonant structures

There are two general types of dissonant structures: those that combine two levels of motion, both of which are based on the division of a time span by a prime number, and those which do not

3. It will be objected here, by those well-versed in mathematics and acoustics, that Fourier analysis has described these kinds of relationships more formally and exhaustively since the mathematics for these kinds of structures do not differ from what is required to describe the interference patterns formed by the combination of sinusoidal waves. This study does not avail itself of this kind of approach because it is interested in what the interference patterns look like when they are slowed down to the rate of typical musical events. At this slower rate meter and syncopation become functions of the interference patterns; they are musical phenomena upon which the higher mathematics do not concentrate. In light of this, the higher mathematics tend to overpower the theory (not to mention the theorist) and do not illuminate, to any greater extent, the aesthetics of rhythm.

satisfy this condition because one or both of the numbers are non-prime. A prime structure includes no other equal divisions of the time span except those of its constituent levels. A partial listing of prime structures appears below. This list is limited to what may reasonably be expected to appear in the context of musical rhythm.

2 against 3	3 against 5	5 against 7	7 against 11
2 against 5	3 against 7	5 against 11	7 against 13
2 against 7	3 against 11	5 against 13	7 against 17
2 against 11	3 against 13	5 against 17	7 against 19
2 against 13	3 against 17	5 against 19	
2 against 17	3 against 19		11 against 13
2 against 19			11 against 17
			11 against 19

5. Non-prime dissonant structures

A non-prime dissonant structure differs from a prime one in one important respect: it is able to include at least one additional level of motion that is consonant to one of its initially constituent patterns. Example 5.5 illustrates this.

```
D:    6            6
C:    4      4        4
B:    3  3       3____3
A:    3  1   2   2  1   3
```

Example 5.5

Level A is 3 against 4, the resultant of the initially constituent patterns shown on levels B and C. Since level B has a non-prime number of attacks, however, it may include a level of motion consonant to it. In this case, the additional level is the halving of the time span shown on level D, and it is easily derived by pairing the elements of level B (lower slurs). Thus the 3 against 4 of level A includes the 2 against 4 formed by levels D and B.

On this basis, level A also includes 2 against 3, since level C interacts with D to create this latter structure. This is shown in example 5.6.

```
C:     6       6
D:     4   4       4
       4   2   2   4
```

Example 5.6

The resultant of C and D (4   2 2   4) may be reduced, by
dividing its time values by their smallest common denominator, to
the easily recognizable form: 2   1 1 2. All of the inclusions of
3 against 4 are now displayed in example 5.7.

```
E:    6               6            2 pulses      ⎫
D:    4       4       4            3 pulses      ⎪
C:    4       2   2   4            2 against 3   ⎬  2 against 4
B:    3   3       3       3        4 pulses      ⎪
A:    3   1   2   2   1   3        3 against 4   ⎭
```

Example 5.7

Note that the slower and included 2 against 3 in the above example may be derived by the groupings indicated by the slurs on
level A. This is equivalent to tying the dotted rhythms of the pattern
in music notation: 4   2   2   4
                    3   1   1   3

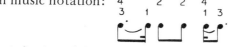

A further elaboration of the 3 against 4 structure is also possible;
its appearance has been seen in Chopin's Opus 34, #3 (example 4.29).
There, the initial and final time values of the 3 against 4 resultant
were split in order to create two further instances of 2 against 3.
This is shown on level A in example 5.8.

```
C: 4           2   2   4            2 against 3
B: 3       1   2   2   1   3        3 against 4
A: 2   1   1   2   2   1   1   2
```

Example 5.8

It should be stressed that level B of the above example includes
level C but does not include level A. Rather, A includes both B

and C. Each individual 2   1 1 2 of level A, however, (see brackets) is a smaller sub-pattern that appears within the longer time span of B and C. It is for this reason that this kind of relationship has been called a nested structure. When considered separately, each 2   1 1 2 is nested within the time span of B and C, but neither of the two instances of 2   1 1 2 includes the slower levels. Level A only includes B and C when it is taken as a whole (2   1 1 2 2   1 1 2).[4]

Like 3 against 4 in the above examples, other non-prime dissonant structures will also include consonant levels of motion and thereby include slower-moving dissonant structures. A partial list of non-prime patterns and the dissonant structures they include is presented below.

2 against 9 includes:
2 against 3

2 against 15 includes:
3 against 5
2 against 5
2 against 3

3 against 4 includes:
2 against 3

3 against 8 includes:
3 against 4
2 against 3

3 against 10 includes:
3 against 5
2 against 5
2 against 3

3 against 14 includes:
3 against 7
2 against 7
2 against 3

3 against 16 includes:
3 against 8
3 against 4
2 against 3

4 against 5 includes:
2 against 3

4 against 6 includes:
3 against 4
2 against 3

4 against 7 includes:
2 against 7

4. It will be seen later that the pattern on level A in example 5.8 is really 4 against 6:

4 against 9 includes:
3 against 4
2 against 9
2 against 3

4 against 10 includes:
4 against 5
2 against 5

4 against 11 includes:
2 against 11

4 against 13 includes:
2 against 13

4 against 14 includes:
4 against 7
2 against 7

4 against 15 includes:
4 against 5
3 against 5
3 against 4
2 against 15
2 against 5
2 against 3

4 against 17 includes:
2 against 17

4 against 18 includes:
4 against 9
4 against 6
3 against 4
2 against 9
2 against 3

5 against 6 includes:
3 against 5
2 against 5
2 against 3

5 against 8 includes:
4 against 5
2 against 5

5 against 9 includes:
3 against 5

5 against 12 includes:
5 against 6
4 against 6
4 against 5
3 against 5
3 against 4
2 against 5
2 aginast 3

5 against 14 includes:
5 against 7
2 against 7
2 against 5

5 against 16 includes:
5 against 8
4 against 5
2 against 5

6 against 7 includes:
3 against 7
2 against 7
2 against 3

6 against 8 includes:
4 against 6
3 against 8
3 against 4
2 against 3

6 against 9 includes:
2 against 9
2 against 3

6 against 10 includes:
5 against 6
3 against 10
3 against 5
2 against 5
2 against 3

6 against 11 includes:

3 against 11
2 against 11

6 against 13 includes:
3 against 13
2 against 13

6 against 14 includes:
6 against 7
3 against 14
3 against 7
2 against 7
2 against 3

6 against 15 includes:
5 against 6
3 against 5
2 against 15
2 against 5
2 against 3

6 against 16 includes:
6 against 8
4 against 6
3 against 16
3 against 8
3 against 4
2 against 3

6 against 17 includes:
3 against 17
2 against 17
2 against 3

7 against 8 includes:
4 against 7
2 against 7

7 against 9 includes:
3 against 7

7 against 10 includes:
5 against 7
2 against 7
2 against 5

7 against 12 includes:
6 against 7
4 against 7
4 against 6
3 against 7
3 against 4
2 against 7
2 against 3

7 against 15 includes:
5 against 7
3 against 7
3 against 5

7 against 16 includes:
7 against 8
4 against 7
2 against 7

7 against 18 includes:
7 against 9
6 against 7
3 against 7
2 against 9
2 against 7
2 against 3

The above list should suffice for indicating the kinds of included dissonant structures that appear within the non-prime dissonant forms. The reader may extend the list by simply inspecting the constituents of a structure (for example, 8 against 9) and listing the consonant levels that each constituent of the structure may include (8 includes 4 and 2; 9 includes 3). The included dissonant structures are formed by the oppositions of the included levels with each other and with the constituents of the original structure (4 against 9, 3 against 8, 3 against 4, 2 against 9, 2 against 3).

6. The inclusion of dissonance within consonant structures

Some of the consonant structures may also include deeper levels of motion that are dissonant either to each other or to the constituent elements of the original consonant structure. A shortened list of these inclusion relationships follows.

2 against 6 includes:
2 against 3

2 against 10 includes:
2 against 5

2 against 12 includes:
4 against 6
3 against 4
2 against 3

2 against 14 includes:
2 against 7

2 against 18 includes:
6 against 9
2 against 9
2 against 3

2 against 6 includes:

2 against 3

3 against 12 includes:
4 against 6
3 against 4
2 against 3

3 against 15 includes:
3 against 5

4 against 12 includes:
4 against 6
3 against 4
2 against 3

5 against 10 includes:
2 against 5

5 against 15 includes:
3 against 5

Again, a continuation of the list is accessible to the reader by the method of inspection described in the paragraph preceding this section.

7. Dissonant structures with 2

The reason for the listings of inclusion relationships that have appeared thus far will be made clearer by an inspection of those dissonant structures in which one of the constituent levels of motion is a bisection of the time span.

2 against 3:
2   1 1 2

2 against 5:
2   2 1 1 2   2

2 against 7:
2   2   2 1 1 2   2   2

2 against 9:
2   2   2   2 1 1 2   2   2   2

2 against 11:
2   2   2   2   2 1 1 2   2   2   2   2

2 against 13:
2   2   2   2   2   2 1 1 2   2   2   2   2   2

2 against 15:
2   2   2   2   2   2   2 1 1 2   2   2   2   2   2   2

2 against 17:
2   2   2   2   2   2   2   2 1 1 2   2   2   2   2   2   2   2

It is logically necessary that a bisection of a time span, when combined with some division of the span based on an odd number, will
result in a pattern that contains an attack at the point of bisection.
This attack cannot, of course, coincide with any of the attacks of an
odd division of the span because the odd divisions will never be
evenly divisible by 2.

The rhythmic result is the consistent nesting of 2 against 3
(2   1   1   2) within any pattern formed by 2 against an odd
number, and this is indicated by underscoring in the above list.
Each of the patterns there may be described as a sequence of regular
pulses that nests within it a 2 against 3 structure.

The implications of this nesting relationship are far-reaching. An
overwhelming number of the non-prime dissonant structures listed
above (and the consonant structures that contain dissonant relationships) can be seen either to include 2 against 3 as a dissonant structure or to present 2 against 3 (in the form of 2 against an odd number) as a nested structure at some level.[5] The only five exceptions are
those structures that ultimately include, instead, 3 against 5 or 3
against 7.

5. The reader can confirm this by inspecting the listed inclusion relationships of sections
5 and 6 in this chapter.

It is no accident, then, that the structure of musical rhythm in a great number of individual compositions is characterized by 2 against 3 as an included dissonant structure or as a nested foreground detail. The structure of the rhythmic system itself, in spite of its vast potential for variety, retains 2 against 3 to a considerable extent as a common element. Again, this is clearly not universal, nor is it a secret source of the coherence of all rhythmic design. It is, however, one of the chief characteristics of musical rhythm, and as such it is a beginning point for reducing the universe of rhythmic configurations down to a conceptually manageable size.

8. The compositional use of nesting

A concrete example of the aspects of rhythm discussed in the preceding paragraph will be helpful here. This example appeared as a problem for rhythmic analysis at the end of Peter Westergaard's essay "Some Problems in Rhythmic Theory and Analysis"[6] (example 5.9).

Primary Segmentation. A primary segmentation of the passage is indicated by brackets below the staff of example 5.9. The clearest segment is marked "Segment III." This phrase has a definitive point of beginning in terms of:

1) The change of density brought about by the doubling instruments (which is equivalent to #2).
2) The point of entrance of new timbres.
3) The point of recurrence of virtually all the musical content that appears as segment IB in the example, including the steady eighth-note foreground rhythm.

By any of the above criteria, the point of detachment between segment III and the music that immediately precedes it is straightforward.

---

6. *Perspectives on Contemporary Music Theory*, p. 226. This piece has also been analyzed by Schoenberg in "Brahms the Progressive," reprinted in *Style and Idea* (New York, 1950), p. 95.

Example 5.9

This is not the case between segments I and II. Either segment II begins with a return to $\hat{5}$ from its upper neighbor (shown as IIB), or it begins after the rest (shown as IIA). In the latter case, the rest functions to detach II A from the immediately preceding material. Segment I likewise has two possibilities. As segment IA it ends before the beginning point of IIA and appears as a long phrase, beginning with the first d, ascending to $\hat{5}$, prolonging $\hat{5}$ with an upper neighbor, and finally returning to $\hat{5}$ in the fourth measure of the example. As segment IB, it ends at the beginning point of IIB—before the return to $\hat{5}$—and the brackets under the example indicate how this form of the segment duplicates segment III.[7]

A closer look at the middleground motions of the individual segments indicates that they are not overly complex. Looking first at segments IA, IB, and III, they each prolong $\hat{5}$ over a pedal tone by means of a chromatic passing tone (*f-sharp*) which leads to an upper neighbor. Segment II introduces the dividing dominant of the whole passage in the form of a $\begin{smallmatrix}6\\4\end{smallmatrix}$ - $\begin{smallmatrix}5\\3\end{smallmatrix}$ suspension.

Individual Levels of Motion and Dissonant Structures. The accentuation of the bass pattern at the beginning of the passage is displayed in example 5.10. The repetition of the low *b-flats* interprets

Example 5.10

7. The criterion used for determining IB and III is the recurrence of $\hat{5}$; i.e., each new instance of $\hat{5}$ begins a new segment. The criterion for determining segment IA is the quarter rest which, again, detaches this segment from IIA. There is no basis, however, for considering segment I to begin at $\hat{5}$ in the first bar but to end with $\hat{5}$ in the fourth bar, since the rhythm from event to event is, in this case, the rhythm from $\hat{5}$ to $\hat{5}$. The second instance of $\hat{5}$ is therefore a new attack-event and not logically connected to the first attack of $\hat{5}$ in bar 1. The only way to include both of these instances of $\hat{5}$ within the same segment is to do so on the basis of some other criterion (the quarter rest). In such a case, the attacks on $\hat{5}$ are not the primary determinants of the segmentation, and therefore segment IA begins not with *f* but rather with *d*. Thus segment IB is a sub-pattern, determined by one criterion, that is contained within a larger sub-pattern determined by another criterion. And this accounts for the two possible forms of segment II.

the rhythm of the foreground in terms of a quarter-note motion (level A). The quarter notes are paired by the first two right-hand attacks. This latter level of motion (half notes) also coincides with the motion from $\hat{3}$ to $\hat{5}$, and it is shown on level B. It may be suggested, then, that a metric scheme on the order of $\frac{2}{8}$ or $\frac{2}{4}$ is established at the beginning of the example. The interaction of the foreground with level A is $\frac{2}{8}$; $\frac{2}{4}$ is the interaction of level A with level B. There is no slower rate of events that groups the half notes of level B in pairs, and so the meter signature of the passage is not musically represented at this point.

In segments IB and III, however, there is a distinctly slower rate of events that groups the quarter notes of level A and the half notes of level B. This slower rate of motion is provided by the middleground events of the upper voice, and it is emphasized by the recurrence of dynamic stresses. Example 5.11 illustrates this slower stratum within segments IB and III on level C.

Example 5.11

In this example level A preserves the quarter-note grouping and level B the half-note grouping that has been established at the beginning of the passage (seen first in example 5.10). Level C now displays the time span of $\hat{5}$ and the time span of its upper neighbor. Each of these tones is effective for a span of five quarter notes. Note that the *sf* markings emphasize the bisection of the five half notes of the passage (level B) into two groups of five quarter notes each (shown by the brackets above level C).

The interaction of levels B and C forms a dissonant 2 against 5 structure, as shown in parentheses in example 5.12. Note how the nested 2 against 3 (2   1   1   2) of this intermediate structure encompasses the chromatic passing tone as well as the upper neighbor.

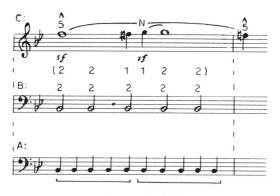

Example 5.12

Mozart's repetition of the phrase with instrumental doubling in segment III clarifies the 2 against 5 even further. In example 5.13, the cello part appears on a level between the middleground motion of level C and the half-note motion of level B. Note how the cello sforzando coincides with the chromatic passing tone leading to the upper neighbor. Thus, although the cello itself presents a stress that recurs at an interval of four quarter notes, this level of motion combines with the dynamic stresses of the other instrumental parts to bring out the essential pitch motion of the upper line and with it the essential rhythmic pattern that controls the segment: a dissonant 2 against 5. The stresses also emphasize the centrally nested 2 against 3 (above the bracket) that is formally a part of the 2 against 5 structure: 2 ⌊2   1   1   2⌋ 2.

Example 5.13

With the recognition of this 2 against 5 sub-pattern the larger segment IA may now be seen to contain it as a nested structure. In example 5.14 the attack pattern formed by the bass grouping of level B and the middleground motion of level C becomes a 2 against 5 (in brackets) with an additional half-note beat at either end.

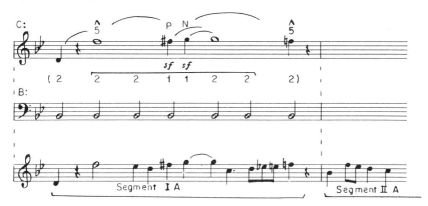

Example 5.14

The entire motion to $\hat{5}$, the chromatic passing tone, the upper neighbor and return to $\hat{5}$ are now constituents of the structure shown in parentheses in the sketch, 2 against 7:
2 2 2 1 1 2 2 2. Furthermore, it can now be seen that the 2 against 5 that is formally nested within 2 against 7 is compositionally isolated from the longer segment (IA) and presented by Mozart in segment III (figure 5.1).

```
                  2 against 5                    -   segment III (and IB)
  | 2    '2    2    1   1   2    2'   2 |         -   segment IA
                  2 against 7
```

Figure 5.1

It must now be asked which of the constituent levels of these dissonant structures is vital to a metric interpretation of the music in these segments: the divisions of the spans into 5 or 7, or the bisections of the spans. Although the dissonance is pitch-structural, a comparative evaluation of middleground levels will not help here. This is because the bisections of the spans are created in each case by a stressed arrival on the upper neighbor *g*, while the alternate divisions of the spans, in terms of half-note motion, are equally important—not only because they reflect the recurrence of the pedal tone but even more because Mozart clearly wishes the *f-sharp* to be accentuated (the additional cello *sf* in segment III), and this *f-sharp* also coincides with the half-note motion.

A look at the abstract form of the third segment clarifies the problem (example 5.15).

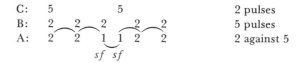

Example 5.15

Level A is 2 against 5, level B is the level of half-note motion, and level C is the bisection of the span. (The upper slurs show the derivation of level C from A; the lower slur, the derivation of level B.) A favoring of either level B or C as a metric indicator requires that either of the two central attacks of level A (1   1) takes precedence. An accent on only the first '1' interprets the pattern of level A as being metrically controlled by level B—with C being a superimposed level of motion (2̌ / 2 / 1 1̌ / 2 / 2). An accent on only the second '1' of the pattern accomplishes the reverse (2̌ 2̌ 1̌ / 1 2̌ 2̌). But since Mozart arranges for these two central attacks to be, effectively, equally weighted, the result is a double accentuation of the structure (2/2/1/1/2/2)—a double interpretation of level A. This is no different from leaving the structure metrically uninter-

preted; neither of the groupings is favored because both are equiv-
alently favored. Hence, there is no meter because both meters are
equally indicated; the rhythmic organization of segments IB and
III is, rather, shaped by an uninterpreted dissonant structure. On
the larger scale, the larger segment IA is coherently organized with
segment III by containing it as a nested structure in terms of the
relationship previously shown in figure 5.1.

The predominance of structurally uninterpreted motion[8] in the
first and third segments is tempered by the metric interactions of
segment II (A or B). This middle segment is a clear return to the
$\frac{2}{4}$ metric groupings that are tentatively established in the first measure of the example (shown in example 5.10). The following sketch
(example 5.16, A and B) indicates that segment IIA is a rising motion
of an inner voice (*b-flat–c*) leading to the *d* below *f* that begins
segment III. The bar lines of segment IIA are placed in the sketch
to conform with the V divider in the bass that bisects the segment,
making the *d* of the $\frac{6}{4}$ suspension an accented passing tone. Segment
IIB does not change this metric reading but merely appends an
additional bar of $\frac{2}{4}$ onto the segment.

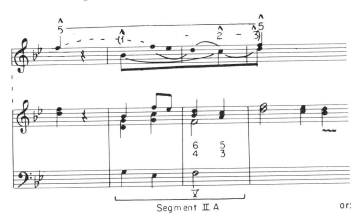

Example 5.16

8. The distinction between this structurally uninterpreted motion and the uninterpreted
patterns first described in chapter 2 should be made clear. An analytically uninterpreted
structure can be found in any rhythmic configuration by simply considering the pattern to
be without accents. In this example, however, the composer has saturated a pattern with
accents, leaving it accentually undifferentiated and thus uninterpreted. This lack of accent is not merely an earlier stage of analysis here; it is also a final stage because of the pitch
structure of the example.

Example 5.16, continued

   The entire passage thus begins with a tentative metric grouping
and returns to metric grouping in segment II. The first and third
segments are predominantly uninterpreted motion, however, and are
organized in terms of related, dissonant intermediate structures. The
importance of nesting in this example can now be completely seen
by observing the foreground detail of segment II: ⌐2   1   1   2⌐ 2.
The nested presence of 2 against 3 in shorter time values integrates
the rhythm of segment II with the structure of I and III, since it is
precisely this sub-pattern that is shared by both 2 against 7 and
2 against 5 (figure 5.2).

			2	1	1	2			−2 against 3—segment II
		2	2	1	1	2	2		−2 against 5—segment III, IB
	2	2	2	1	1	2	2	2	−2 against 7—segment IA

Figure 5.2

   Finally, a rhythm-to-pitch examination of the rhythm of the
melodic line reveals a further integration of the 2 against 3 structure; this line progressively utilizes first the trisection and then the
bisection of the same time span. Note, in example 5.17, how the
attack-point rhythm gives equal value (4) to the more stable events
of the middleground ($\hat{5}$–N–$\hat{5}$). The intervening motion between these
greater-valued events can be seen to divide the span of six eighth

notes first into 2+ 2 +2 and then into 3 + 111, thus exploiting the structure of 2 against 3 horizontally.[9]

With the exception of this last observation, which discovers 2 against 3 as a function of different levels of motion based on 2 and 3, none of the other appearances of the 2   1 1 2 structure in this

Example 5.17

example are compositionally used in this way; nor are they included within other dissonant patterns in the sense that inclusion has been defined in this chapter. Instead, the structural basis of this example is almost exclusively an outgrowth of the nesting relationships displayed in figure 5.2; and although these relationships do not exhaustively describe the rhythm of the example, they are its coherence.

9. Dissonant structures formed by skipped levels

The dissonant and consonant structures presented thus far in this chapter have been generated in terms of a division relationship. They are formed by the opposition of two different regular divisions of the same time span. As indicated in chapter 1, however, division is only one way to describe a rhythmic phenomenon. The same dissonant relationships may be equally well described as the interaction of two different rates of motion, or as the interaction of two separate strings of attacks in which the regularly recurring attacks of each individual string have a fixed duration (or attack-point interval) different from that of the attacks of the other string.

The latter two approaches are a more dynamic way of looking at

9. It is perhaps this attack-point opposition of 2 2 2 with 3 1 1 1 that prompted Schoenberg to rebar the music in the following way, making each of these patterns a different interpretation of a bar of $\frac{3}{4}$:

dissonant structures, since the various strings of durations (or the two rates of motion) need not be restricted to any particular time span, but rather may be allowed to continue for any length of time. Example 5.18 illustrates this. The 3 against 4 pattern (bracketed in A) analytically describes a pattern that will cyclically recur if B and C are extended indefinitely, but the motions of B and C need not stop in an individual composition simply because one cycle of the structure (3   1 2   2   1 3   ) has been completed.

```
C:    4       4       4      4     4
B:    3    3      3       3    3  3
A:    3    1 2   2    1 3    3    1 2
```

Example 5.18

Most of the dissonant structures discussed in this chapter have also been presented in terms of adjacent levels of motion (2 and 3; 3 and 4, etc.). This is demonstrated on levels A through E in example 5.19. (Each level of regular motion is a string of durations measured in quantities of sixteenth notes.)

```
F:    8                       8

E:    4          4        4          4
D:   (3     1 2    2    1 3)    (3
C:    3        3      3       3       3       3
B:   (2  1 1  2)  (2  1 1  2)  (2   1 1
A:    2   2      2   2   2     2    2    2
```

Example 5.19

Here levels A and C are adjacent, and level B is formed between them. Likewise levels C and E are adjacent, and D is formed between them. Suppose, however, the rhythm of a musical work is metrically organized such that attacks of level E are grouped in pairs by events on the slower level F. It is altogether possible in such a case that the individual motion on one of the levels not adjacent to F will interact with the motion on level F without any musical representation of the intervening levels. A dissonant pattern formed in the above example by opposing these non-adjacent, or skipped levels, appears below.

```
                            F:    8                    8
                            C:    3    3    3
            new pattern:         ⌐ 3    3    2 ⌐ 8
```

Example 5.20

In example 5.20 the 3 3 2 pattern is the result of the interaction of levels C and F because the intervening motion on level E has been skipped. With the rate of events on C opposed only to the rate of events on F, one of the commonest rhythmic patterns of the world's music is produced. This pattern has often been incorrectly assumed to be "additive" because it contains unequal time values.[10] Yet no explanation could lead further away from the nature of the above structure than this term because, in spite of the fact that the structure is truncated, it still is the result of two different regular rates of motion. Here 3 3 2 is clearly a disguised form of the dissonant structure of level D—disguised by the absence of the second '4' of level E because, again, level E has been skipped (i.e., the 4s of level E are tied in pairs).

The traditional samba pattern uses precisely this relationship formed by skipped levels. It is metrically organized in terms of level F, but the motion of level C (3 3 3) is recurrently superimposed on the slower pattern. Example 5.21 illustrates first the superimposition of the motion of level C at the point of each new event of level F.

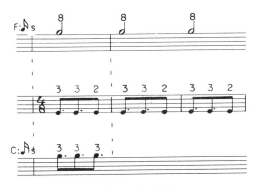

Example 5.21

10. Curt Sachs describes 3+3+2 as only an additive rhythm on p. 94 of *Rhythm and Tempo* (New York, 1953).

Note how the first three attacks of the pattern formed between
levels C and F are really the rate of recurrence on level C. With the
true metric indicator being the events on F, however, the motion on
level C is abbreviated at the end of each bar, only to be reinstated at
the beginning of the next bar.

The samba makes a more intensive use of this relationship. It may
be seen as the 3 3 2 pattern followed by its retrograde (2 3 3),
with the 2s tied together. The result is that the end of one samba
pattern (2 3 3) is followed by the beginning of the next (3 3 2),
and the rhythmic scheme becomes highly syncopated because the
superimposed level of motion (C) extends for five attacks in a row
(3 3 3 3 2). Example 5.22 shows this aspect of the pattern in
brackets. Again, it should be stressed that the fundamental structure
of the example is not simply an additive succession of equal and
unequal values but is, rather, a dissonant relationship between two
nonadjacent strata, C and F, each of which is characterized by
equal-valued motion.

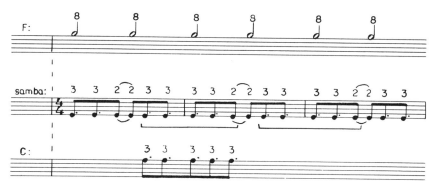

Example 5.22

10. Internal properties of dissonant structures

When multiple levels of regular motion are combined and extended,
the resultant patterns that cyclically recur will have two retrograde
properties that really are aspects of the same relationship. The first
is an identity between any resultant and its own retrograde. The
following examples illustrate this general property. The retrograde
of each pattern will duplicate the pattern (example 5.23).

3 against 5:	3	2	1 3	1 2	3			
4 against 7:	4	3	1 4	2 2	4	1 3	4	
5 against 6:	5	1 4	2 3	3	2 4	1 5		

Example 5.23

The basis of this aspect of each whole pattern is the internal retrograde within each pattern. There are two types of this internal relationship. In 3 against 5, neither constituent of the pattern is evenly divisible by two, and so there is no attack that bisects the pattern. As a result, the central attack (3) is shared by each segment of the pattern. It is the final attack of the opening segment of the pattern (3 2 1 *3*) and the first attack of a closing segment that is a retrograde of the opening (*3* 1 2 3). The other patterns in example 5.23 are clearly bisected by an attack in each case, and so the first half of the attacks of each pattern is followed by a retrograde of itself, which becomes the second half of each pattern.

Metric accentuation may either emphasize or disguise this internal retrograde relationship. A representation of 2 against 3, for example, may either ignore the internal retrograde:

2   /1 1/2

or may bring it out:

2   1/1 2

11. Large-scale properties of dissonant structures

The word structure has been used in three ways in this study. First, it has signified the presence of any purposeful organization; to have structure in this sense is to have order. Second, works of music have been viewed as structures in the aesthetic sense. When taken as a whole, each composition is a unique ordering of rhythmic values and is hence a unique structure.

This section addresses itself to a third aspect of rhythmic structure: the one that has appeared most often in the previous chapters. In this third sense, structure is a logical and generalized set of relationships. This can be demonstrated by examining the large-scale properties of 3 against 4. This pattern includes the constituent rates: 2, 3, and 4. As such, it includes the consonant relationship of 2 against 4 and the dissonant 2 against 3. In effect, a fuller description of the structure that takes all of these levels into account is 2 against 3 against 4.

With this fuller structure, a further set of relationships may be elaborated by deriving the patterns that will include 2 against 3 against 4. These additional patterns are easily found by opposing one of the constituent levels of motion within 2 against 3 against 4 (3, for instance) against a level of motion posited by multiplying the values of the other constituent levels by each other (in this case, 2 X 4. The additional pattern is thus 3 against 8). Doing this three times for 2 against 3 against 4 is a simple way of determining that the pattern will be included in 3 against 8, 4 against 6, and 2 against 12. With the addition of the levels of motion based on 6 and 8, the pattern is also therefore included in 6 against 8 and 8 against 12.

Thus 3 against 4 is the nexus of a whole family of relationships. It includes:

> 2 against 4
> 2 against 3

It is included in:

> 4 against 6
> 3 against 8
> 6 against 8
> 2 against 12

Example 5.24 is a display of this large-scale rhythmic structure organized about 3 against 4.

```
I:         12                  12                          = 2
H:    ▲     8          8                 8                 = 3
G:   in     8          4      4          8                 = 2 against 3
   cluded                                                  > 2 against 4
F:   │      6          6                 6           6 ────── = 4
E:         │6│       2 4        4      2   6               = 3 AGAINST 4
D:    ▲     4     2  2 4        4      2 2   4             = 4 against 6
C:   in     3  3     2 1 3      3      1 2 3      3        = 3 against 8
   cluding  3     1 2  2  1 3   3      1 2 2 1 3           = 6 against 8
B:   │
A:    ▼    2 1 1 2     2    1 1 2 2 1 1 2   2     1 1 2     = 8 against 12
```

Example 5.24

In the example above, the nexus of the structure is enclosed in a box. The included levels are displayed above the box. The including levels are displayed below the box. Finally, the nested forms of 2 against 3 on levels D and A, and 3 against 4 on level B, are underlined.

The elaboration of this family of abstract inclusion relationships makes it again possible to render the variety of rhythmic design more manageable conceptually. This is due precisely to the transitive properties that obtain between levels of the large-scale rhythmic structure. In example 5.24, E includes F,G,H, and I; C and D include E; thus, C and D include F,G,H, and I. Since C and D are included by B and A, these latter structures also include E,F,G,H, and I. Seeing the logical architecture of a large-scale rhythmic structure may thus be a way of elucidating a complex nexus pattern in terms of a simpler included or including pattern.

For example, 2 against 3 against 5 (6   4   2 3   3   2 4   6) may be understood as the nexus of a larger structure.

2 against 3 against 5 includes:	3 against 5	
	2 against 5	
	2 against 3	

It is included in:	5 against 6	6 against 10
	3 against 10	10 against 15
	2 against 15	6 against 15

Thus 5 against 6, 3 against 10, and 2 against 15 all share a complex sub-pattern (2 against 3 against 5), but they reflect a relationship between three levels of motion (2, 3, and 5) in terms of a relationship between two levels of motion (5 and 6, or 3 and 10, or 2 and 15). One of these relationships (2 against 15) is a simple dissonant structure with 2. As such, it nests the same pattern that is formed by an included level (2 against 3), and this pattern, as a nested and included configuration, is far simpler than the complex resultant of 2 against 3 against 5. These simpler patterns do not exhaustively describe the complexity of the nexus patterns. Quite to the contrary, they allow non-unique aspects of complex patterns to be made visible.

There is no limit to the number of levels of regular motion that may be combined and investigated in this way. For instance, 2

against 3 against 5 against 7 is more amenable to analysis as a pattern
that is included within 10 against 21, or 14 against 15, or ultimately
within 2 against 105 (which again must be simply a series of regular
attacks within which is nested a 2   1 1 2 pattern). Furthermore,
the transitive property of large-scale rhythmic structures guarantees
that 10 against 21 has a logical relationship to 14 against 15, and
these patterns, too, are reducible to the 2 against 3 of the extreme
included dissonant pattern or the nested 2 against 3 of the extreme
including dissonant pattern.

All of these large-scale rhythmic structures are available to musical
compositions which then represent one or more of their levels as
accentuated and meter-defining motion, or as uninterpreted motion,
or as syncopated motion arising out of the superimposition of one
regular level upon the accentuated events of another regular level.

The rhythmic foregrounds of compositions are thus transformed
by interpretive middleground rhythmic levels. Indeed, the meaning
of a rhythmic foreground is determined by the deeper middleground
rhythmic structures it contains and by the kinds of interaction
these deeper structures display with each other or with the foreground. In addition, each of these deeper structures can be viewed
not only in terms of itself but also in terms of a family of inclusion
relationships to which it belongs. The composition, in turn, may
generate now one, now another pattern belonging to the same
family. And, although the patterns may appear to be different
from each other, the inclusion relationships of the large-scale rhythmic structure remain in force at the deeper levels and lend their
formal coherence to the composition.

Because of the nature of this formal coherence, a composition may
very often unfold a rhythmic pattern in the same way that it un-
folds a pitch interval. Example 5.25, A shows a typical unfolding
third. The descent of a third, indicated by quarter notes, nests
within it a duplicate of itself, indicated by the slurred, unattached
noteheads. The rhythmic levels of example 5.25, B (taken from the
large-scale structure of 3 against 4) are unfolded in precisely the
same way. The middleground structure of level G nests a duplicate
of itself, underlined on level D; numerous examples of just this kind
of rhythmic unfolding have been observed in chapter 4 of this study.

Example 5.25

Thus, as the unfolding interval is a reflection of the formal nature of a tonal system, so too is the unfolding rhythmic configuration a reflection of the abstract inclusion relationships of a rhythmic system.

Other large-scale rhythmic structures may be derived by the reader using the same techniques discussed in this section. As mentioned earlier, these structures carry the coherence of their logical organization into compositions that utilize them.

6

Problems in the
Construction of a General
Theory of Rhythm

Extreme caution should be exercised in evaluating the universality
of a theory. If it is too specific to a small domain of musical phenomena, a theory may mistake the unique aspects of very few
compositions for general principles. On the other hand, if the theory
is too general, the degree to which it may illuminate specific problems may be marginal when compared with the effort expended in
arriving at general principles and solutions.

In this light, the useful applications of the theoretical principles
and analytic procedures described in the preceding chapters would
appear to be limited to a kind of tonal music in which the middleground rhythmic levels exhibit some regularity of motion. Although
it applies on these terms to a vast repertory of compositions, the
theory described in this study is therefore by no means general.[1]

It may appear at first blush that ritardando, accelerando, and
tempo rubato instructions are the kinds of phenomena that inter-
fere with regular motion and thus present problems for the theory,
but this is not the case. If meter were misunderstood to be solely a
foreground phenomenon, then a gradual slowing down of a pulse
on the surface of a composition would have the effect of dissipating
all semblance to regular motion. But since meter has been defined as
a relationship between levels, this dissipation does not occur.

Suppose, for example, that there is a $\frac{4}{4}$ metric interaction between
Foreground A and Middleground B such that the events on B occur

---

1. I mention this limitation in the context of Western music. The rhythmic practices of
sub-Saharan African drum orchestras and Balinese and Javanese orchestras also depend
to a great extent upon the mutual opposition of different levels of regular motion. For these
non-Western musical cultures, the large scale structures described in chapter 5 are indeed
applicable and are helpful to analysis.

once for every four regular attacks on A. It is important to see that the stratification of rhythm in such a case is simultaneous. If a ritard slows down the foreground, it slows down the middleground; if tempo rubato distorts the regularity of the foreground, the middleground is similarly distorted, but the linkage between levels is undisturbed. The four-to-one relationship between foreground events and those of the middleground will be sufficiently preserved for the metric interaction to remain functional between the levels. Thus the metric regularity of several bars of $\frac{4}{4}$ may be schematically unchanged in spite of the fact that a ritard alters the motion for the purposes of expression. Rhetorically, there is in fact a rhythmic alteration, but structurally, the phrase may still be treated as containing regular motion.

Far more serious problems for a general theory of rhythm have been presented by two common characteristics of music that has been written during the present century. First, there is the kind of composition that appears to exhibit absolutely no regularity of motion on any level. This can be caused by either of two conditions: the music is exactly what it appears to be in that there is nothing in it resembling a pulse; or the music is so saturated with conflicting rates of regular motion that it is purposeless to begin to specify any of them, since they obscure each other utterly.

The only analysis that this study can offer this type of rhythmic texture is a rhythm-to-pitch examination of attack-point patterns that may possibly recur on the foreground. Such an approach can be augmented by the discovery of additional significant sub-patterns on the basis of timbre, dynamics, density, and register in accordance with the techniques and principles described in chapter 2.

Second, there is the problem of middleground pitch levels in atonal music. There is no reason to suppose that pitch middlegrounds in atonal composition, if they exist, will have the slightest resemblance to those of tonal music; if anything, to concentrate on the coloristic presence of tonal-like structures (in Berg, for example) is the surest way to obscure the nature of a predominantly atonal style.

Yet in spite of the fact that seeking tonal prolongations in atonal compositions is somewhat like looking for Gothic arches in Renaissance churches, there is some basis for suggesting that a middleground of sorts may be present. Presumably, not every pitch in an atonal

composition is equally weighted. Some pitches appear more frequently than others, and some appear to embellish while others
seem more stable. Since there is no general pitch theory for discov-
ering these middleground structures, however, a pitch-to-rhythm
analysis of an atonal composition seems impossible to formulate
at this time.

An alternate, albeit highly tentative, project might apply the
techniques of rhythm-to-pitch analysis to atonal music. With such a
solution, some of the formal aspects of large-scale rhythmic structures might allow the discovery of atonal, middleground pitch strata
on the basis of rhythmic hierarchies. This approach provides a cir-
cuitous route to the middleground pitches, since they are posited
on the basis of middleground rhythmic patterns.

A composition that appears potentially amenable to this technique
is Schoenberg's Opus 23, no. 2. The opening bars are displayed in
example 6.1.

Used by permission of Edition Wilhelm Hansen

Example 6.1

It is not clear, however, that the upbeat scheme which Schoenberg
has notated will necessarily survive in live performance. Example 6.2
presents the same pitches in a rhythmic notation based on their
attack points. Note that the three regular events on the lower staff
mark off the events of the upper line in groups of four. Against this,
Schoenberg has beamed the sixteenth notes to suggest an initial
group of three. The relationship between the pitch sequences that
correspond to this possible partitioning of the sixteenth notes in
both threes and fours is a 3 against 4 structure—which may be considered uninterpreted. It is also possible that one of the groupings
may be considered metrically operative.

Example 6.2

There has been room here for only the most general suggestion of the above approach. The point of mentioning it is not so much to achieve an immediate solution as it is to formulate the problem in a new and potentially solvable way; i.e., to approach middleground pitch levels in atonal music via middleground rhythmic levels. This kind of reformulation of traditional problems that appears in this study has, no doubt, given rise to as many questions as it has answered. It has, nevertheless, provided a language in which the following concluding statements can be made:

1) Procedurally, the relationship between pitch and rhythm can only be understood non-circularly either by valuing some of the attacks within a rhythmic pattern because they coincide with important pitches, or by valuing certain pitches because they coincide with recurrences of important rhythmic patterns.
2) Music without rhythmic accent is still characterized by rhythmic structure—uninterpreted structure—especially when the musical rhythm consists of unique sequences of attack-point intervals.
3) In terms of pitch-to-rhythm procedure, the single most important source of a rhythmic accent in tonal music is the presence of a significant, middleground pitch event. Patterns of poetic feet, as Hauptmann declared, are "the outside of the edifice" of rhythm. The accents within these patterns are themselves reflective of events that appear on deeper strata of purposeful motion, these latter being the slower, middleground pitch levels.
4) Meter is defined as a relationship between two different strata of equal-valued motion that are consonant to each other. It re-

quires both a faster and a slower pulse and results from the conceptualized interaction of the two.

5) The rhythm of tonal music is unambiguously metric if a middleground level of regular motion is implied by middleground pitch-events to be of clearly singular importance.

6) If two purposeful middleground levels interact, rhythm may be syncopated—with syncopation being understood as a dissonant or displaced level of motion that is strongly superimposed upon a continuing scheme of metric accent. This accent will be determined by the more structurally significant of the middleground pitch levels. In lieu of being pitch-structural, the superimposed level of motion may originate with stresses.

7) If two conflicting rates of middleground motion have their origins in different middleground pitch levels of truly equivalent structural importance, a single metric accentuation of the foreground may be impossible to determine. In such a case, the foreground rhythm is structurally uninterpreted. Neither metric interaction is functional because both are functional.

8) As an uninterpreted structure, the attack-point pattern of two conflicting and dissonant rates of motion is equivalent to the resultant of the rhythmic conflict expressed as a single line of rhythm. This equivalence gives rise to the aesthetic coherence of the rhythmic structures of many tonal compositions, since their foreground attack-point sequences are very often isomorphic to patterns that are formed on or between their middleground levels.

9) Foreground rhythmic patterns consisting of notes of equal and unequal values are not always best described as additive patterns, since they may very often have, as their source, deeper middleground levels that are characterized by only equal-valued motion.

10) Any configuration that is made up of levels of regular motion can be seen in the context of a family of transitively related patterns. As a large-scale rhythmic structure, such family relationships provide a logical ground for many of the internal isomorphisms that individual compositions display.

The ultimate implication of the present study has special import for the theory of tonality itself. It would appear that any general definition of tonality made exclusively on the basis of pitch and pitch function is, in and of itself, incomplete. Tonality requires a rhythmic component, since it is created by middleground spans and arpeggiations interacting with foreground configurations in accordance with certain obligatory rhythmic relationships. In this sense, Heinrich Schenker's theory of pitch levels is, fundamentally, also a theory of rhythm.

It is hoped that the above conclusions have some relevance to an eventual construction of a general theory of rhythm—one that can comprehend the aesthetics of complex motion within unique works of art in a mode that is intrinsically musical.

Bibliography

BOOKS

Alette, Carl. "Theories of Rhythm." Diss., Eastman School of Music, 1951.

Anonymous IV. "De Mensuris et Discantu." CS 1: 327 ff.

Cooper, Grosvenor and Meyer, Leonard B. *The Rhythmic Structure of Music.* Chicago, 1960.

Erikson, Raymond F. "Melodic Structure in Organum Purum: A Computer Assisted Study." Diss., Yale University, 1970.

Feil, Arnold. "Satztechnische Fragen in den Kompositionslehren von F.E. Niedt, J. Riepel, und H. Chr. Koch." Diss., Heidelberg, 1955.

Garlandia, Johannis De. "De Musica Mensurabili Positio." CS 1: 97 ff., 175 ff.

Haenselman, Carl Ferdinand. "Harmonic Rhythm in Selected Works of the Latter Half of the Nineteenth Century." Diss., Indiana University, 1966.

Hauptmann, Moritz. *The Nature of Harmony and Meter.* Trans. W.E. Heathcote. London, 1888.

Heinichen, Johann David. *Der General-Bass in der Composition.* Dresden, 1728.

Jerome of Moravia. "Discantus Positio Vulgaris." CS 1: 94 ff.

Kirnberger, Johann Philipp. *Die Kunst des reinen Satzes in der Musik.* Berlin, 1777.

Mattheson, Johann. *Der vollkommene Capellmeister.* Hamburg, 1739.

Mursell, James L. *The Psychology of Music.* New York, 1937.

Odington, Walter. "De Speculatione Musici." CS 1: 182 ff.

Perkins, Marion Louise. "Changing Concept of Rhythm in the Romantic Era . . . ." Diss., University of Southern California, 1961.

Pierce, Anne Alexandra. "The Analysis of Rhythm in Tonal Music." Diss., Brandeis University, 1968.

Plato. *Republic.*

_____. *Timaeus.*

Riemann, Hugo. *Geschichte der Musiktheorie im IX–XIX Jahrhundert.* Leipzig, 1898.

_____. *Musikalische Dynamik und Agogik.* Hamburg, 1884.

_____. *System der musikalischen Rhythmik und Metrik.* Leipzig, 1903.

Riepel, Joseph. *Anfangsgründe zur musikalischen Setzkunst.* Regensburg, 1754.

Sachs, Curt. *Rhythm and Tempo.* New York, 1953.

Schenker, Heinrich. *Das Meisterwerk in der Musik.* Jahrbuch I. Munich, 1925. Jahrbuch II. Munich, 1926. Jahrbuch III. Munich, 1930.

_____. *Neue musikalische Theorien und Phantasien.* Vol. 1. Vienna, 1906. Vol 2. Vienna, 1910. Vol. 2, 2. Vienna, 1922. Vol. 3. Vienna, 1935.

Schillinger, Joseph. *The Schillinger System of Musical Composition.* New York, 1946.

Schoenberg, Arnold. *Style and Idea.* New York, 1950.

Smither, Howard Albert. "Theories of Rhythm in the Nineteenth and Twentieth Centuries." Diss., Cornell University, 1960.

Sowa, Heinrich. *Ein anonymer glossierter Mensuraltraktat 1279.* Konigsberg, 1930.

Waite, William G. *The Rhythm of Twelfth Century Polyphony.* New Haven, 1954.

Wedge, George H. *Rhythm in Music: A Textbook.* New York, 1927.

Westphal, Rudolph. *Allgemeine Theorie der musikalischen Rhythmik seit J. S. Bach auf Grundlage der Antiken.* Leipzig, 1880.

Williams, Charles Francis Abdy. *The Aristoxenian Theory of Musical Rhythm.* Cambridge, England, 1911.

ARTICLES

Anderson, Warren. "Word Accent and Melody in Ancient Greek Musical Texts." *JMT* 17, no. 2 (1973), pp. 186 ff.

Beach, David. "A Schenker Bibliography." *JMT* 13, no. 1 (1967), pp. 2 ff.

Cazden, Norman. "The Principle of Direction in the Motion of Similar Tonal Harmonies." *JMT* 2, no. 2 (1958), pp. 162 ff.

Forte, Allen. "Schenker's Conception of Musical Structure." *JMT* 3, no. 1 (1959), pp. 1 ff.

Jackson, George Pullen. "The Rhythmic Forms of the German Folk Songs." *Modern Philology* 13 (1915–16): 561 ff.; 14 (1916–17): 65 ff.; 15 (1917–18): 79 ff.

Lennenberg, Hans. "Johann Mattheson on Affect and Rhetoric in Music." *JMT* 2, no. 2 (1958), pp. 193 ff.

Lewin, David. "A Metrical Problem in Webern's Op. 27." *JMT* 6, no. 1 (1962), pp. 125 ff.

Palisca, Claude V. "Vincenzo Galilei's Counterpoint Treatise: A Code for the Secunda Pratica." *JAMS* 9, no. 2 (1958), pp. 81 ff.

Stetson, Raymond B. "Teaching of Rhythm." *MQ* 9 (1923): pp. 181 ff.

Westergaard, Peter. "Some Problems in Rhythmic Theory and Analysis." Reprinted in *Perspectives on Contemporary Music.* Edited by Benjamin Boretz and Edward T. Cone. New York, 1972.